To God's beloved people who will read this book, please note that all of the scriptures in Bold is Jesus speaking to you. Please, take the time to listen as He imparts His word into your Spirit.

As we all know, there are hundreds if not millions of authors that have written devotionals over the years. It is my belief that no one has written one quite like this. This devotional is for you to read one day of the week and allow the Holy Spirit to resonate in you that which has been spoken by Him. We all beloved, have an area or areas in our lives where we are "weak" and that is why the Holy Spirit has lead me to write this devotional. This book will speak to the very core of our spirits and help each of us to realize how very important it is for us to maintain an intimate relationship with our Savior. It tells us who we are in Christ, how to change some of our worldly habits, and it assures us of God's continual and unconditional love for us no matter who we are, or what we have done.

The enemy is the only one who continues to make us think that we are not worthy of God's forgiveness, mercy and grace. That is why I am encouraging you not to rush through this book. Most of us read a devotional each day - and that is fine, however, we are sometimes so busy that we do not allow the word to penetrate. With this book, however, you can chose whatever day is more convenient for you to spend time reading so that you can digest each written word. I believe that you will not regret it and that it will make a tremendous impact on your life and on the lives of those which you chose to share it with. Be blessed as you turn each week of trials into triumph. -Mrs. A. Morgan

A Word for Your "Weak"

MRS. A. MORGAN

WESTBOW
PRESS®
A DIVISION OF THOMAS NELSON
& ZONDERVAN

This book is a work of non-fiction. Unless otherwise noted, the author and the publisher make no explicit guarantees as to the accuracy of the information contained in this book and in some cases, names of people and places have been altered to protect their privacy.

WestBow Press books may be ordered through booksellers or by contacting:

WestBow Press
A Division of Thomas Nelson & Zondervan
1663 Liberty Drive
Bloomington, IN 47403
www.westbowpress.com
1 (866) 928-1240

Because of the dynamic nature of the Internet, any web addresses or links contained in this book may have changed since publication and may no longer be valid. The views expressed in this work are solely those of the author and do not necessarily reflect the views of the publisher, and the publisher hereby disclaims any responsibility for them.

Any people depicted in stock imagery provided by Thinkstock are models, and such images are being used for illustrative purposes only. Certain stock imagery © Thinkstock.

ISBN: 978-1-5127-8507-4 (sc)
ISBN: 978-1-5127-8509-8 (hc)
ISBN: 978-1-5127-8508-1 (e)

Library of Congress Control Number: 2017905946

Print information available on the last page.

WestBow Press rev. date: 9/21/2017

Acknowledgements

First and foremost I want to thank my Lord and Savior for His mercy, grace, wisdom, understanding and insight that He put on the inside of me. Without Him, this book would not have come to pass. I also want to express a great gratitude and love for my husband, Mike. You have been my best friend, cheerleader and support system through this whole ordeal. Thank you for allowing me the endless amount of time that I spent locked in my office and trying to labor through the birth of this devotional. Your patience, love, longsuffering, encouragement, and belief in me upheld my arms and gave me the will to continue. Without you, it would have not been possible to get through some of the most frustrating times that I have experienced. And, of course there is all of you at WestBow Press who diligently and patiently edited, merged, and made awesome suggestions to enhance this publication. However, a special thanks with my heart bowed to Mrs. Rita Moore - the very first person that contacted me from WestBow. Although it was more than a year after our initial contact; you never gave up on me. I thank God for your patience, not pressing and for our many conversations in which you encouraged me before this long process began. I am forever grateful for each one of you, without you and your part there would be no completion.

WEEK 1

Are We Just Moving, or Are We Moving with Compassion?

John's disciples came and took his body and buried it. Then they went and told Jesus. When Jesus heard what had happened, he withdrew by boat privately to a solitary place. Hearing of this, the crowds followed him on foot from the towns. When Jesus landed and saw a large crowd, he had compassion on them and healed their sick. (Matt. 14:12–14 NIV)

It is my belief that Jesus had just as many concerns and heartaches as we have today. In Matthew 14:13, it says that when Jesus heard that John had been beheaded, he withdrew to a place of solitude. I can only imagine that Jesus's heart must have been broken. Yet when the crowds followed Him, Jesus had compassion and was moved to heal their sick.

I know that there are times when we all desire to go to a place of solitude, and there always will be, but we too must be moved with compassion for others as they come into our space and require us to listen, pray, or give a word of encouragement or hope to help them get through their trials.

Sometimes it is hard to give a word of comfort when you are hurting yourself. However, what we give out will be reciprocated back to us. When we are in pain from this life's trials and tribulations, ultimately that is the perfect time to heal another soul. Let's remember that compassion moves us to do something for someone else; therefore, it plays a big role in our everyday lives. We should do our best to live by the example that Christ left for us. Until next time, make it a blessed week.

WEEK 2

What Are You Carrying to God?

Cast your cares on the LORD and he will sustain you; he will never let the righteous fall. (Ps. 55:22 NIV84)

I was recently reminded by a friend of mine of an old spiritual hymn, "What a Friend We Have in Jesus." The song says, "All our sins and grieves to bear, what a privilege to carry everything to God in prayer. Oh what peace we often forfeit, oh what needless pain we bear, all because we do not carry everything to God in prayer."

Beloved, in the society in which we live, unfortunately, we want quick fixes, not permanent solutions. Therefore, we will not carry our problems, no matter how big or small, to Jesus because we must wait for Him to answer. The verse above says *cast* your cares. That word means "to throw down in a sudden motion, to hurl, to let go of," but how many of us are doing that? Exactly what are we carrying to God?

We know without a shadow of doubt that we do not have the wisdom to fix our cares ourselves without the help of our Heavenly Father, yet because of our _wills_ we refuse to cast them to the one person who can and will sustain us. He promises that He will never let the righteous fall. Won't you take Him at His word today and cast all of your cares upon the Lord and, this time, leave them there. Until next time, make it a blessed week.

WEEK 3
Overflowing with Confident Hope

I pray that God, the source of hope, will fill you completely with joy and peace because you trust in him. Then you will overflow with confident hope through the power of the Holy Spirit. (Rom. 15:13 NLT)

People of God, we can overflow with confident hope simply because we have a sure foundation in Jesus. We know that His love for us will take us and keep us no matter what. No matter where you might be today or in what situation you find yourself, you and I can trust and rely on the God of hope to fill us with joy and peace. He has a peace that surpasses all understanding.

I truly realize that life can sometimes throw us a curve ball, but that does not mean that we have to catch it. Throw it back and give the devil a black eye. Jesus is the source and power of our entire hope. Put your trust in Him and believe only what He has to say about us and our circumstances. *There is nothing too hard for God.*

Ask God as the scripture says above to completely fill you with joy and peace simply because you trust in Him. You and I have power through the Holy Spirit. The devil does not want us to tap into that power, but God does. So go ahead, overflow today with confident hope knowing that God will give you the grace to face whatever challenge and trial you have today and every day. Until next time, make it a blessed week.

WEEK 4

Have You Been with Jesus Today?

The members of the council were amazed when they saw the boldness of Peter and John, for they could see that they were ordinary men with no special training in the Scriptures. They also recognized them as men who had been with Jesus. (Acts 4:13 NLT)

Beloved, as you and I prepare to start our days and our to-do lists, do we stop long enough to get dressed for others to recognize that we have been with Jesus? In our world of busyness, getting the children or grandchildren off to school, preparing lunches, thinking about our meetings and lunch appointments, putting a load of laundry in the washer before rushing out the door, making that quick phone call to set up an appointment for a loved one, or whatever it is that we do, we should stop first to spend time with our Lord and Savior.

I have found that when I honor, *"But seek ye first the kingdom of God, and his righteousness; and all these things shall be added unto you," (Matt. 6:33 DARBY)*, my day goes a lot smoother than even I expect. We all live extremely busy lives, but we cannot afford to *not* pencil God into our schedules. None of us know what our days will entail and who God intends for us to meet. We are always on assignment because we are all ministers of the Gospel. Therefore, we should try to be prepared to complete our unknown assignments each day.

The Bible tells us that Peter and John were just ordinary men with no special training in scriptures; therefore, we are without excuse to clothe ourselves with God's word on a daily basis. As we prepare for the rest of our weeks, let's take the time to put on our armor so that others will know we have been with Jesus. Until next time, make it a blessed week.

A Word for Your "Weak"

WEEK 5

Despite What You Think Your Inabilities Are, Will You Say Yes?

Brothers, think of what you were when you were called. Not many of you were wise by human standards; not many were influential; not many were of noble birth. But God chose the foolish things of the world to shame the wise; God chose the weak things of the world to shame the strong. He chose the lowly things of this world and the despised things—and the things that are not—to nullify the things that are, so that no one may boast before him. (1 Cor. 1:26-29 NIV84)

I can only speak for myself, but there are times when I feel incomplete, with no ability at all to do an assignment that has been given to me by the Lord. I often ask Him, "Lord, why did you choose me for this assignment? It is way out of my comfort zone." However, I quickly come to myself and realize that God knows me better than I will ever know myself. He knows what He put into me and how to get it out of me, and He knows the same thing about each of you.

God would not call any of us to do something that He has not already preordained for us to do. He promises in His word, *"For I know the plans I have for you,' declares the LORD, 'plans to prosper you and not to harm you, plans to give you hope and a future"* (Jer. 29:11 NIV).

We have to learn to continue to trust God with every aspect of our lives. That is indeed a process; however, it can be done. God said that *He chose*. It was His choice to call the foolish things to shame the wise and the weak things to shame the strong. Therefore, when we are feeling weak or unwise, we need to praise God for choosing us to complete an assignment for Him. He could have chosen anyone, my beloved, but He chose us. What an amazing God we serve!

So the next time you are faced with a challenging assignment that you feel is too great for you, remember that you have been chosen by the almighty God and say yes. Until next time, make it a blessed week.

WEEK 6
In The Waiting

In the morning, O LORD, you hear my voice; in the morning I lay my requests before you and wait in expectation. (Ps. 5:3 NIV84)

We all have many requests and things that we desire from our Lord and Savior. I suppose the question is how long are we willing to wait for an answer? It still amazes me how some people, even those of us who are devout Christians, will wait in line for all kinds of objects and new toys. The newest iPhone, iPad, tablet, toys for our children—the list goes on and on. When the stores have a special on that TV for Black Friday, we are the first ones to get there and we stand in line for hours and hours in the cold just to get a bargain.

But how long will we stand to hear an answer from the Lord to a request that we put before Him? Usually, if He takes too long, we immediately begin to institute plan B, C, G, H, K, and so on. We do not want to wait on the Lord and be of good courage. Unfortunately, the option to wait does not exist for some of us. We want instant gratification and immediate answers from the Father, who knows best for each of us.

The next question is if, and I did say *if*, we are waiting, how are we waiting? Are we really waiting with expectancy, knowing that God will answer, or do we have an attitude, anger, frustration, doubt, or worry? It really does matter how our posture is as we wait on the Lord for His divine purpose to be fulfilled in our lives. As we continue to lay our requests before the Lord, let's learn to wait in expectation, knowing that when the time and season is right, He will answer.

Until next time, make it a blessed week.

WEEK 7
How Is Our Faithfulness?

"Whoever can be trusted with very little can also be trusted with much, and whoever is dishonest with very little will also be dishonest with much. (Luke 16:10 NIV)

Are we faithful and trustworthy in the small things God has called us to do? What about the job we currently have? Are we doing it to the best of our abilities and unto the glory of God? Do we get up every morning wishing we did not have to go to that workplace, not realizing that there is someone who would just love to have a job so that they could fulfill their obligations? Can God trust us to go the extra mile, or are we doing the bare minimum, just enough to get by? Do we feel that the job we have is beneath us and that we deserve much better than this?

Beloved, I am by no means saying that our work is always pleasant. Neither am I saying that those we work with or for are loving, kind, considerate, or right. However, I am saying that God already knew who, where, and what you and I would be doing, yet He allowed us to be placed there for His purpose. Can we be trusted over the little so that we can obtain the much?

Our promotions are oftentimes predicated on whether or not we are faithful where we are. It may be in our workplaces, our ministries, our neighborhoods, our homes, etc. We may feel that we deserve that promotion, and perhaps we do, but how is our trust where we are?

Faithfulness to God is an option. We can choose to exhibit it wherever we are and in whatever circumstances we find ourselves, or we can choose to ignore it and not gain the success that God has for each of us. It really is our choice. God's word tells us that if we cannot be trusted with little, then we will not be trusted with much, and if we are dishonest with little, then we will be dishonest with much.

Let's take a leap of faith and remain faithful to the one who keeps us every day. Until next time, make it a blessed week.

WEEK 8

God Will Hang Your Enemy on what They Prepared to Hang You On!

All the royal officials at the king's gate knelt down and paid honor to Haman, for the king had commanded this concerning him. But Mordecai would not kneel down or pay him honor. Then the royal officials at the king's gate asked Mordecai, "Why do you disobey the king's command?" Day after day they spoke to him but he refused to comply. Therefore they told Haman about it to see whether Mordecai's behavior would be tolerated, for he had told them he was a Jew. When Haman saw that Mordecai would not kneel down or pay him honor, he was enraged. Yet having learned who Mordecai's people were, he scorned the idea of killing only Mordecai. Instead Haman looked for a way to destroy all Mordecai's people, the Jews, throughout the whole kingdom of Xerxes. Then Queen Esther answered, "If I have found favor with you, O king, and if it pleases your majesty, grant me my life—this is my petition. And spare my people—this is my request. For I and my people have been sold for destruction and slaughter and annihilation. If we had merely been sold as male and female slaves, I would have kept quiet, because no such distress would justify disturbing the king." King Xerxes asked Queen Esther, "Who is he? Where is the man who has dared to do such a thing?" Esther said, "The adversary and enemy is this vile Haman." Then Haman was terrified before the king and queen. The king got up in a rage, left his wine and went out into the palace garden. But Haman, realizing that the king had already decided his fate, stayed behind to beg Queen Esther for his life. Just as the king returned from the palace garden to the banquet hall, Haman was falling on the couch where Esther was reclining. The king exclaimed, "Will he even molest the queen while she is with me in the house?" As soon as the word left the king's mouth, they covered Haman's face. Then Harbona, one of the eunuchs attending the king, said, "A gallows seventy-five feet high stands by Haman's house. He had it made for Mordecai, who spoke up to help the king." The king said, "Hang him on it!" So they hanged Haman on the gallows he had prepared for Mordecai. Then the king's fury subsided. (Esther 3:2-6, 7:3-10 NIV)

Beloved, you may be going through a trial in your life right now that seems as if it is going to hang you. It was designed to take you out. However, you and I must be assured that nothing and no one can out do God. He has His hands on us, and all things are working for our good. You may be facing a challenging time in your workplace, in your marriage, with your children, with your parents, or in another relationship. But, if you hold on and hold out, God will hang your enemy and entrap him or her in what he or she planned for you.

We must continue to stay focused and walk in faith and the love of God, no matter what the enemy brings our way. We are more than conquers, divinely appointed for such a time as now. Encourage yourself and make a conscious decision to do as Mordecai did; do not bow to anything or anyone that is not of God and be willing to fight for what is right. We are God's chosen, and He makes no mistakes about the assignments He gives us to complete. He knows that we are already equipped to handle the battle; we just need to know it. God does not call the equipped, He equips the called.

Remember to stay steadfast and unmovable in every aspect of the plan that God has for you. We may not understand it all right now, but in the end we will win. Let's just wait and watch while God hangs our enemy right where he or she planned to hang us. God bless and Until next time, make it a blessed week.

WEEK 9

How Do You View Your Workplace?

Whatever you do, work at it with all your heart, as working for the Lord, not for men, since you know that you will receive an inheritance from the Lord as a reward. It is the Lord Christ you are serving. (Col. 3:23–24 NIV)

Well, my beloved, while I realize that I am not physically in the workplace of corporate America anymore (and neither are some of you), no matter what our day-to-day lifestyles might be, we are all living in a spotlight. We are being watched wherever we go and whatever we do. How we view where we are will determine our attitude toward our places of work. Trust me when I tell you that someone is always watching, especially when we confess Jesus as Lord of our lives.

Our places of work may be different, but our conduct should not be. Even if we are in our home offices answering e-mails or a telephone call, we should do it as unto the Lord. We never know how much our lives depict Christ, even through our telephone conversations or the tone of our e-mails. The other person on the end of the line might be experiencing a difficult time when you or I speak with him or her. That coworker in the break room might be admiring how well you handle stress and conflict on the job. He or she may need to glean from you and mimic how you act or speak.

As the summer months approach, perhaps you work where there will be interns or young people who come in to give a hand. Let's try to remember that we are to be a positive influence in the lives of God's people. We do not want to be a stumbling block, especially to our young people, by demonstrating an attitude of ungratefulness for the job and provisions that God has allowed us to have. I realize that some things in our everyday life situations might get a little tough. At those times, take a *Jesus break* and then come back working with all your heart because we are working unto the *Lord!* Until next time, make it a blessed week.

WEEK 10
Do You Recognize the Voice?

Again the LORD called, "Samuel!" And Samuel got up and went to Eli and said, "Here I am; you called me." "My son," Eli said, "I did not call; go back and lie down." Now Samuel did not yet know the LORD: The word of the LORD had not yet been revealed to him. The LORD called Samuel a third time, and Samuel got up and went to Eli and said, "Here I am; you called me." Then Eli realized that the LORD was calling the boy. So Eli told Samuel, "Go and lie down, and if he calls you, say 'Speak, LORD, for your servant is listening.'" So Samuel went and lay down in his place. The LORD came and stood there, calling as at the other times, "Samuel! Samuel!" Then Samuel said, "Speak, for your servant is listening." (1 Sam. 3:6-10 TNIV)

In our above scripture, Samuel did not yet know the Lord; therefore, he could not recognize His voice. But what about us? With so many voices speaking at one time, do we recognize which is the voice of the Lord?

Unfortunately, we live in a society in which everybody is trying to get our attention. Voices are all around us. Some are loud, some are soft, some are squeaky, some are sad, and the list goes on. However, the question is this: Are we listening for the soft, quiet voice to speak to us in the midst of all the other chatter? When it does, will we recognize His voice?

Because life has many demands and we are torn in many directions during the progress of our day, it is definitely a challenge to tune our spirits to hear the Holy Spirit as He gives us directions and instructions for the choices and decisions that we make. Beloved, believe it or not, we cannot make it without Him. Only He knows what the next second holds for each of us. Sometimes our thoughts are all over the place, wondering what to say or not to say, what to do or not to do, which way to go or not to go, and so on. But we have to learn to *be still* long enough to hear the right voice that will guide us to where He has already destined for us to be.

The old adage that says practice makes perfect is a good one to grab hold of and keep until we are assured that we recognize His voice. Today, let's practice being still so that we too can say, "Speak, Lord, for your servant is listening." Until next time, make it a blessed week.

WEEK 11

Sometimes It Takes a Painful Praise!

Dear friends, do not be surprised at the painful trial you are suffering, as though something strange were happening to you.

But rejoice that you participate in the sufferings of Christ, so that you may be overjoyed when his glory is revealed. If you are insulted because of the name of Christ, you are blessed, for the Spirit of glory and of God rests on you. If you suffer, it should not be as a murderer or thief or any other kind of criminal, or even as a meddler. However, if you suffer as a Christian, do not be ashamed, but praise God that you bear that name. (1 Pet. 4:12-16 NIV84)

With all that is going on in our world today, just getting up and leaving our homes is an effort, and going anywhere can sometimes be an exhausting experience. But I have good news for you and me. God already knows the trials, tribulations, and circumstances that you and I face and has already made a way of escape. Somebody shout hallelujah! Thank God that nothing surprises Him and nothing is strange to Him. He is well aware of what is going on in each of our lives and is capable of handling all of them simultaneously and without error.

God does not just wake up in the morning, look at one of His children, and let out a loud shout of surprise because He did not know the next chapter of his or her life. The Bible states above that we are not to be surprised by the painful trials as if something strange is happening to us. It also says that we are to rejoice in the sufferings of Christ.

I know, I know. I can hear you saying, "You don't know my story. How do you expect me to rejoice in this mess?" Beloved, sometimes it takes a painful *praise* to help us get through to the next level of our growth in Jesus. Remember, **from everyone who has been given much, much will be demanded, and from the one who has been entrusted with much, much more will be asked** (Luke 12:48 NIV). We want to acquire stuff without going through anything to ascertain it, but that, my beloved, is not an option we can choose. When the pressures come and the pain is intensified, just know, as the scripture says, that you and I are bearing the name of Christ and we are not to be ashamed.

Let's take time out and render a painful praise unto the Lord, for He alone is worthy. Until next time, make it a blessed week.

WEEK 12

Does It Seem as if the Wall Won't Move?

Therefore this is what the LORD says: "If you repent, I will restore you that you may serve me; if you utter worthy, not worthless, words, you will be my spokesman. Let this people turn to you, but you must not turn to them. I will make you a wall to this people, a fortified wall of bronze; they will fight against you but will not overcome you, for I am with you to rescue and save you," declares the LORD. "I will save you from the hands of the wicked and deliver you from the grasp of the cruel." (Jer. 15:19–21 TNIV)

Beloved, some walls are in place in our lives for our own good and protection, yet often we scream and fight for the wall to come down and for us to be released. Instead of viewing the wall as an object of protection, we see it as an obstacle that we cannot get through, over, around, or under. Some walls are in place to shield us from the very attempts of the Antichrist. How we are viewing the wall is out of focus. We want to see what is behind that wall; we want to know what is there while God is trying to shield us from the very elements that are lurking in danger to entrap us.

As precious children of God, we must learn to take our hands off certain situations and circumstances and leave them in the capable hands of a loving Father. He is our protector. Learning to trust God for the wall and leaving it in place will be an ongoing process for us to accomplish. Some of us must learn that it is on a need-to-know basis and there will always be things that we do not need to know. God will not reveal everything to us simply because we want to know it. He knows what we can and cannot handle and when, where, and how much to reveal to us on any given day and in any given situation. So the next time you or I are facing a wall that seems as if it will not come down, let's view it as a fortress to protect us and not as an obstacle that we cannot move. Until next time, make it a blessed week.

WEEK 13

Can You Praise God for What You Don't See?

Let everything that has breath praise the LORD! Praise the LORD! (Ps. 150:6 ESV)

God desires for us to praise Him, because His word says: *"Let the whole world bless our God and loudly sing His praises" (Ps. 66:8 NLT)*. However, because life can sometimes be hard, we do not offer praise to God when we are going through life's storms. Quite often we are angry and frustrated, confused and unavailable for the use of our Heavenly Father. We tend to shut ourselves off from the world and go into our hiding places where no one and nothing can penetrate our spirit, not even God Himself.

Just like we know there is wind and cannot see it or when sitting in a chair have confidence that it will hold us, we must be confident that God has a plan and that it is working for our good. Let's not want to be pitied and prayed for and for someone else to truly understand the hard thing we are facing; instead, let's go ahead and praise God in the midst of it.

Praise, my beloved, changes the atmosphere. It puts our faith to work and scatters the enemy and his imps. The devil does not expect us to praise God for what we cannot see; however, when and if we can, it confuses him and he must leave. Remember, it is written, "Resist the enemy and he will flee." When it looks like everything in your world is tumbling down and all hope is gone, praise God in spite of it. Ask Him to open your Spiritual eyes and take a look into the heavenly realm and shout for what is taking place on your behalf.

I am not saying this is easy. There are and still will be many times that I must put on praise and worship music just to lift myself from where the enemy is trying to entrap me. It takes practice, but it does work. When we can learn to praise God for what we do not see, the manifestations of what is really there will appear. Until next time, make it a blessed week.

WEEK 14

No Matter What, God Is Compassionate!

The thought of my suffering and homelessness is bitter beyond words! I will never forget this awful time, as I grieve over my loss. Yet I still dare to hope when I remember this: The faithful love of the LORD never ends! His mercies never cease. Great is his faithfulness; his mercies begin afresh each morning. (Lam. 3:19-23 NLT)

As I read the scriptures above, I indeed can relate to Jeremiah about the thoughts of suffering and homelessness, as probably can some of you. It is not easy to grieve over loss and at the same time remember that we serve a compassionate God.

As we go through our daily lives and see, hear, or read the devastating reports of so many losses that our world suffers, one might ask, where is God in all of this? That question really comes to mind when tragedy hits too close to home or knocks at our front door. However, my beloved, God is still a God of compassion, and His love for us will never end. Who else loves us so much that they would allow us to do whatever we choose for as long as we choose to do it, even when they *know* it is not good for us and could possibly cause us more harm than good? Only a Heavenly Father of unconditional love who has given us free will but is always there to welcome us back into His grace.

Every morning we have an opportunity to make correct choices and try again to live better lives for Jesus. There is no one else who loves us enough to give us new mercies every day to start all over again. It is my belief that we should take some time this week to reevaluate our lives, right this minute, right where we are in life, and reconsider our choices. God wants to extend His compassion toward us, so let us reach out to Him and accept it. He is a restorer of all things. His mercies never cease, and they are *NEW* every morning.

Until next time, make it a blessed week.

WEEK 15

An Arm to Lean On

And the LORD said unto Moses, Now shalt thou see what I will do to Pharaoh: for by a strong hand shall he let them go, and by a strong hand shall he drive them out of his land. And God spake unto Moses, and said unto him, I am JEHOVAH: and I appeared unto Abraham, unto Isaac, and unto Jacob, as God Almighty, but by my name JEHOVAH I was not known to them. And I have also established my covenant with them, to give them the land of Canaan, the land of their sojournings, wherein they sojourned. And moreover I have heard the groaning of the children of Israel, whom the Egyptians keep in bondage; and I have remembered my covenant. Wherefore say unto the children of Israel, I am Jehovah, and I will bring you out from under the burdens of the Egyptians, and I will rid you out of their bondage, and I will redeem you with a stretched out arm, and with great judgments. (Exod. 6:1-6 RV)

I can only speak for myself, but there are many times that I need an arm to lean on. When it seems like my world is turning upside down and I am loosing focus and faith, I need to be reassured that there is an outstretched arm available just for me.

I do not know where life finds you today or what your needs might be; however, I do know that you can depend on our mighty Jehovah to bring you through every trial and tribulation you encounter. God hears our every groan and knows our very thoughts even before we think them. Beloved, that is good news!! He promises to keep His covenant with us, even though we have broken ours with Him. Our beloved Father is a promise keeper.

Life is sometimes really hard, and there are questions that will always remain unanswered on this side of Heaven, but God promises to bring us out of every burden and bondage in which the enemy attempts to put us in. Only a mighty arm can give us that assurance of knowing that we cannot lose and that we have already won the battle. Perhaps you know someone in your life or will meet someone this week who needs an arm to lean on. Will you extend yours? It may not be as strong as the arm of our Lord, but it can be used for those whom God allows to cross our paths.

Before we need an arm, let's extend one. Until next time, make it a blessed week.

WEEK 16

We Are Written on the Palms of His Hands!

Yet Jerusalem says, "The LORD has deserted us; the Lord has forgotten us." "Never! Can a mother forget her nursing child? Can she feel no love for the child she has borne? But even if that were possible, I would not forget you! See, I have written your name on the palms of my hands. Always in my mind is a picture of Jerusalem's walls in ruins. (Isa. 49:14-16 NLT)

Sometimes, my beloved, life can take its toll on us, even the very best of us who try hard to think positively, be cheerful, laugh, smile, and speak life daily. There are times when we feel drained and without hope, if only for a few minutes. It is good to know that God has our names written on the palms of His hands. Nothing can touch us there. We are safely hidden, and nobody can pluck us out of the hands of our Heavenly Father.

This is good news to me because I sometimes need reassurance that God would never forget me. We claim to always be strong and never allow anything to hurt or disturb us, but the truth of the matter is that we all have weak moments. Your moments or mine may not be as frequent as those of someone else we know; however, we need to admit to others that we do have some weak moments, just like they do, and then inspire them to go on.

There are people who watch us daily and who have concluded that we are a tower of strength and will always be that way. I am in no way suggesting that we go around gloomy and downhearted—that is not what God would have us to do as Christians who are called to inspire our brothers and sisters—but we can be truthful with those whom God has planted in our presence. We need to share with them that we are assured of being written in the palms of God's hands and that is why we can bounce back so quickly when we experience a moment of weakness.

Is there a name we need to write on the palms of our hands today to remember to pray for him or her, or call, or send an e-mail, or drop by? Perhaps God is nudging you to remember a person you have not seen or talked with in a while. Let them know today that just as Jesus would never forget us, they are not forgotten.

Until next time, make it a blessed week.

WEEK 17
Do We Care Enough to Supply the Need?

You have no reason to fear a sudden disaster or the destruction that comes to the wicked. You can trust the LORD to protect you. He will not let you fall into harm. Do everything you possibly can for those who need help. If your neighbor needs something you have, don't say, "Come back tomorrow." Give it to him immediately. (Prov. 3:25-28 ERV)

Beloved God promises that we as His children have nothing to fear when we hear about disasters or destructions; He will not allow harm to come to us. However, He does expect us to do whatever we can for those in need. I realize, of course, that none of us can always do what we would like for those we hear about, simply because there is so much hurt and so many problems in our world today. But I suppose my question for me and for each of you is this: Are we doing what we can for those who have a need? Are we asking God to let us know what we can do, no matter how small or insignificant it may seem to us?

When I heard about the people in Oklahoma and the disaster they encountered, I wondered, *Lord, what can I do to possibly help?* Then I heard on the news about Channel 4 setting up a phone line for individuals who wanted to pledge for those people. I then thought, *We really don't have resources to pledge, not a substantial amount, anyway.* Then God allowed me to hear one of the people who were accepting pledges and they said that a little ninety-year-old lady pledged ten dollars and that would supply formula and diapers for some of the little ones.

People of God, it is not about the size of our gifts but our obedience to give. When we are led by the Spirit of Christ, we can all supply a need for someone. It may not always be a financial need; perhaps it is a hug, a prayer, a word of hope, or just a smile. We will never know how much it does or how much it was appreciated until we give it. So today I challenge you and me: When we hear of a need—and we will—do all we possibly can to supply it. God will be pleased with each of us.

Until next time, make it a blessed week.

WEEK 18
Do We Need Proof that God Sent Us?

Then Moses answered the LORD, "But suppose the Israelites do not believe me and will not listen to what I say. What shall I do if they say that you did not appear to me?" So the LORD asked him, "What are you holding?" "A walking stick," he answered. The LORD said, "Throw it on the ground." When Moses threw it down, it turned into a snake, and he ran away from it. Then the LORD said to Moses, "Reach down and pick it up by the tail." So Moses reached down and caught it, and it became a walking stick again. The LORD said, "Do this to prove to the Israelites that the LORD, the God of their ancestors, the God of Abraham, Isaac, and Jacob, has appeared to you." (Exod. 4:1-5 GNB)

Let's ask ourselves a question: When was the last time that you or I just did what God asked us to do without wavering about the task? *God, are you sure you want me to do this? What if no one believes me? Suppose I cannot get through to them. But that is not my area of expertise. I cannot just walk up in there and begin to tell those people what they should or should not be doing.* Does any of that sound familiar? I don't know about you, but it sounds familiar to me, and as a matter of fact, the shoe fits, so I am wearing it. Moses was the same way: suppose, Lord, this happens, and if that does happen, then what?

Beloved, God knows exactly what He is doing and who He needs to use for every assignment. Thank God that it is based not on our capabilities but His. We sometimes feel so incompetent, insecure, or unequipped for the tasks that are put before us. However, we should allow God the opportunity to use us as He pleases. Please trust me when I tell you that *if He has called us to it, He will equip us through it.*

God does not give us a task without His enablement. He promised He would never leave or forsake us; we just need to surrender our wills to Him and trust Him in the process. I know there might be times when this is easier said than done; however, we should recall the scripture that says *I can do everything through Christ who strengthens me* (Phil. 4:13 GW).

The next time we are asked to do something for Christ, remember that it is an honor simply because He can use anything or anybody else, but He chose you or me. Only He knows what He put on the inside of us to be used for His glory. Let's stop asking God for proof and, as Nike says, "Just Do It." Until next time, make it a blessed week.

WEEK 19

Do We Have a Steadfast Determination?

As soon as they heard the sound of rams' horns, flutes, lyres, harps, and three-stringed harps with all other kinds of instruments, all the people from every province, nation, and language bowed down and worshiped the gold statue King Nebuchadnezzar had set up. After that happened, some astrologers came forward and brought charges against the Jews. They addressed King Nebuchadnezzar, "Your Majesty, may you live forever! Your Majesty, you gave an order that everyone who hears the sound of rams' horns, flutes, lyres, harps, and three-stringed harps playing at the same time with all other kinds of instruments should bow down and worship the gold statue. Your order said that whoever doesn't bow down and worship will be thrown into a blazing furnace. There are certain Jews whom you appointed to govern the province of Babylon: Shadrach, Meshach, and Abednego. These men didn't obey your order, Your Majesty. They don't honor your gods or worship the statue that you set up." Then, in a fit of rage and anger, Nebuchadnezzar summoned Shadrach, Meshach, and Abednego. Immediately, they were brought to the king. Nebuchadnezzar asked them, "Shadrach, Meshach, and Abednego, is it true that you don't honor my gods or worship the gold statue that I set up? When you hear the sound of the rams' horns, flutes, lyres, harps, and three-stringed harps playing at the same time with all other kinds of instruments, will you bow down and worship the gold statue I made? If you don't worship it, you will immediately be thrown into a blazing furnace. What god can save you from my power then?" Shadrach, Meshach, and Abednego answered King Nebuchadnezzar, "We don't need to answer your last question. If our God, whom we honor, can save us from a blazing furnace and from your power, he will, Your Majesty. But if he doesn't, you should know, Your Majesty, we'll never honor your gods or worship the gold statue that you set up." (Dan. 3:7–17 18 GW)

We can be determined and steadfast about a lot of things; however, how determined and steadfast are we concerning the things of God? Are we consistent in reading His word daily? What about prayer? Is there a determination in that area of our lives? Do we take time during our busy work schedules to thank God before we eat breakfast or lunch or to encourage a coworker or a loved one? In our busy worlds today, little thought goes into what we should be doing for the King. It is my belief, and I did say *my* belief, that we are more consumed with the latest gadgets, iPhone, tablet, or hairstyle that has come out.

Shadrach, Meshach, and Abednego had a determination that compelled them to go beyond and above the call of duty. They stood before the king and took their chances of dying in the fiery furnace rather than defile our Lord and Savior. I cannot speak for anyone else, but I desire that kind of determination to do that which God has called me to do. It amazes me the things that we do stand fast for, and yet not stand when it comes to the things of God. Some of us will not be moved from our normal routines and plans for the day and we do not desire that change.

God desires for us to have a steadfast attitude when it comes to Him. Remember, He wrote in His word: *"So then, my beloved brothers, be steadfast, immovable, always abounding in the work of the Lord, knowing that your labor is not in vain in the Lord"* (1 Cor. 15:58 EMTV). Let's ask ourselves, are we sitting in our business meetings, listening to conspiring ideas of how to wrongly treat others and not speaking up, or are we overhearing a coworker discuss a company policy with someone who is not supposed to know about it?

God is everywhere and with each of us at all times. He sees and hears everything that we do, say, or do not do or say. It is our responsibility to take a stand for righteousness, no matter the cost. Remember, Jesus gave His very life. What are we willing to give?

Until next time, make it a blessed week.

WEEK 20
What Have We Entrusted to God?

For God saved us and called us to live a holy life. He did this, not because we deserved it, but because that was his plan from before the beginning of time—to show us his grace through Christ Jesus And now he has made all of this plain to us by the appearing of Christ Jesus, our Savior. He broke the power of death and illuminated the way to life and immortality through the Good News. And God chose me to be a preacher, an apostle, and a teacher of this Good News. That is why I am suffering here in prison. But I am not ashamed of it, for I know the one in whom I trust, and I am sure that he is able to guard what I have entrusted to him until the day of his return. (2 Tim. 1:9-12 NLT)

People of God, have we truly entrusted everything to our Lord and Savior? That is a question that we need to stop and ponder. Answer it truthfully, not haphazardly just so you can say that you answered it. Give it some time and ask the Holy Spirit to reveal the truth in your heart today.

It is my belief—and I know I say that often, but it is true—that we do not entrust all things to God at all times. I was talking recently with a family member, and we were discussing an issue that occurred with one of their children. As I listened to her and tried to offer some godly wisdom, what I heard was this: "I do not want to see my child go through this circumstance because of the consequences that might occur." Although I repeatedly told this family member that we cannot be our children's God or enabler, it seemed like she did not get the message.

There are times, and will be many, many more, when God will not allow us to intervene on behalf of our children, friends, husbands, wives, or other family member simply because He wants them to come to Him and not to us. Why, I wonder, do we have such a difficult time trusting God with every detail, nook, and cranny of our lives and our loved ones? God is more aware of what is going and what will happen, and He will always know exactly what to do and how to do it. Nothing, my beloved, takes Him by surprise. He can handle our lives simultaneously without any effort.

Believe me, I am by no means suggesting that we should not try to help in ways that we are allowed to; what I am suggesting is that we take a Jesus break to ask the Holy Spirit for directions concerning the situation. When we read about the sufferings of the disciples, apostles, and kings of the Bible, we really cannot compare our circumstances with theirs. They endured trials that will never come our way because of the Blood that Jesus shed for us, yet they trusted God to deliver them. Why then can't, or won't, we? Let's trust God with every detail of our lives today and give our weary souls a rest.

Until next time, make it a blessed week.

WEEK 21
There Is a Greater Power Among Us!

"Be strong and courageous. Do not be afraid or discouraged because of the king of Assyria and the vast army with him, for there is a greater power with us than with him. With him is only the arm of flesh, but with us is the LORD our God to help us and to fight our battles." And the people gained confidence from what Hezekiah the king of Judah said. (2 Chron. 32:7-8 TNIV)

Well, my beloved of God, I can only speak for myself, but I thank God that I can be strong and courageous and not afraid when the enemy thinks he is sending an army out to attack me. It is comforting to know that there is a greater power with me than with him. Sometimes, we need to encourage our own selves through life's storms. Life can and will be hard from time to time, and it may even look as if we are losing the battle, but we can rest assured that God has our backs; the enemy is defeated, and we will win in every situation that we encounter.

No matter who we are or how strong we might think we are, every once in a while the enemy sneaks in and catches us unaware. When that happens, don't lose faith or be discouraged. The battle is already won, and the devil is truly defeated. You may have a circumstance in your life right now that seems insurmountable, but be aware that it is no surprise to God. He already knew it was coming, and He allowed it. Our Heavenly Father knows exactly what to allow and when. He has no doubt that we have gained the power and wisdom to successfully conquer the enemy. We are the ones who need to gain the assurance that if God allowed it, then it is going to work for our good.

As you go through your week and perhaps encounter a trial or tribulation that seems impossible, just remember that there is *a greater power among us*. That power, my beloved, cannot be forced out. Until next time, make it a blessed week.

WEEK 22

Holy Spirit, Take Our Tongues and Help Us Surrender Them to You!

In the multitude of words sin is not lacking, But he who restrains his lips is wise (Prov. 10:19 NKJV). For we all stumble in many things. If anyone does not stumble in word, he is a perfect man, able also to bridle the whole body (James 3:2 NKJV).

Wow! Are we speaking a multitude of words that have sin connected to them?

Our words can be like sharp knives; they cut deep. Even if we go back and apologize and repent to the offended, we cannot take back what we have said. Our body language and tone play an important part in every conversation as well and can leave great pain for the victim to handle. Parents sometimes destroy their children by the words that they speak. I know that I have been guilty of that and pray that I will allow the Holy Spirit to have my tongue so that I will not continue to hurt those I love most.

We may have repented or apologized for the comments we made, but we are not able to remove the sting or scar that was left behind. Only the Holy Spirit has the power to do that. Unfortunately, many families have been torn apart for decades because of a harsh word spoken in a heated discussion. Beloved, we must practice restraining our lips from speaking harsh words, even to that co-worker who has gotten on the only nerve we thought we had left. Or whether it be a rude cashier or your son, daughter, grandchild, husband, wife, sister, or brother. It will not be justified before God on our judgment day as a reason to cause pain to others.

All of us people of God are indeed fallible. We will make mistakes, and some of them will be great. I am a firm believer that practice makes perfect, or at least as perfect as we can be in our unsaved fleshly state. If we try hard enough, we can succeed in becoming people who will think about the words that we speak before speaking them. Why not try to implement that practice today? Before we speak, let's pray and ask the Holy Spirit to help us surrender our tongue to Him. It will only take a minute to win.

Until next time, make it a blessed week.

WEEK 23

Lord, Give Me the Keys

I will give you the keys of the kingdom of heaven; whatever you bind on earth will be bound in heaven, and whatever you loose on earth will be loosed in heaven. (Matt. 16:19 NIV)

Beloved, do you believe that we have the keys to the kingdom of heaven? With those keys at our disposal, we can have anything that we want. Some of us ask God every day to release blessings that are already rightfully ours. We allow trials and tribulations to enter into our lives that we actually have complete control over. We can, if we choose to open our mouths, bind these things on earth and they will be bound in heaven.

That seems easier said than done, but it is that simple. Let's take the summer storms that repeatedly occur. If we would use the power and authority of our words, we could stop the destruction. I for one will use what has been given to me, and I have seen it work. We took the authority and spoke into the atmosphere and declared that the storms stop with no damage to our neighborhood, and it did! Halleluiah!

The devil does not want us to know the power that lies within us so that he can keep us from speaking into the atmosphere. The word clearly states, *whatever you bind.* People of God, that word *whatever* means anything, no matter what. It does not matter what it is; we as sons and daughters of the highest can bind it or loose it.

I realize that we did not earn the authority, we do not deserve it, and we certainly cannot pay for it; however, it still belongs to us. It is my prayer that we will learn to use the keys of the kingdom and to perform kingdom tasks here on earth. My question to all of us is this: why have the keys if we are not going to use them? If we were given keys to our dream home or car, we would use those. Or if we were given the key to a vault that contained millions of dollars, we would indeed use it. So why not use our heavenly keys?

People of God, let's start binding and loosing circumstances in our lives and the lives of others that we love and watch the power of God take over our lives totally for the Kingdom of Christ. Until next time, make it a blessed week.

WEEK 24
Can We Endure Our Light Affliction?

16 So we do not lose heart. Though our outer self is wasting away, our inner self is being renewed day by day. 17 For this light momentary affliction is preparing for us an eternal weight of glory beyond all comparison, 18 as we look not to the things that are seen but to the things that are unseen. For the things that are seen are transient, but the things that are unseen are eternal. (2 Cor. 4:16–18 ESV)

Affliction. I took the opportunity to look up the word in the dictionary, and some of the meanings are suffering, difficulties, problems, pain, etc. I can only speak for myself, but for the most part, I do not like to encounter affliction. The suffering, pain, problems, and difficulties can sometime seem endless. Then, without warning, I get a Spirit check. What about what Christ experienced for me? Can my momentary discomfort compare to His suffering? Would anyone else really die in my place? Those, my beloved, are questions that we all need to ask ourselves from time to time as we face everyday trials and circumstances.

We cannot afford to lose heart. There are those depending on you and me, and we have not yet met them. They are waiting for us on the sidelines of our journey, meant to be passed by so that a divine encounter can be made. If we give up and give in now, those who are assigned to us might die, and we would be responsible; their blood would be on our hands. No one else can complete our assignments and purposes but us. God did not give the anointing to anyone else because He knows what He put in us and for whose purpose. The following should be our prayer: "Father, help us to see the things that are eternal, not temporary, and to work toward those goals with due diligence."

What earthly things are we doing that really have an eternal impact in the lives of God's people? Think about that for just a moment, and allow those words to resonate in your spirit. We are being prepared for eternal glory, and we need to look at our light afflictions through spiritual eyes, knowing that all things are working for good for us because we have been called according to His purpose. That, my beloved, gives us reason enough to endure our light afflictions. Until next time, make it a blessed week.

WEEK 25
What Are We Spending God's Resources For?

Come, all of you who are thirsty. Come and drink the water I offer to you. You who do not have any money, come. Buy and eat the grain I give you. Come and buy wine and milk. You will not have to pay anything for it. Why spend money on what is not food? Why work for what does not satisfy you? Listen carefully to me. Then you will eat what is good. You will enjoy the richest food there is. Listen and come to me. Pay attention to me. Then you will live. I will make a covenant with you that will last forever. I will give you my faithful love. I promised it to David. (Isa. 51:1–3 NIRV)

Beloved, sometimes we need to examine our checking accounts and checkbooks. This is not always something we desire to take a look at, but when we do, we will see exactly what's closest to our hearts. All of us, of whom I am chief, overspend on things that we do not need, just to satisfy a temporary desire that we have for whatever we want at that moment or place in our lives. I personally call it a quick fix shopping tantrum. We can get frustrated or tired of the same old clothes, shoes, television, car, or cell phone in a matter of months and sometimes weeks or days.

Just pick one thing that you quickly wish to change, and if the shoe fits, you need to put it on. With the technology and constant advertisements that are coming in our direction each day, it is difficult to stay close to God's lips and hear Him as He quietly speaks to us on what we really need to do with His resources. Unfortunately, some of us have not reached the place in our Christian walk where we realize that all that we have and accomplish comes from God. Without His strength, knowledge, wisdom, favor, mercy, and grace, we would not have the jobs or resources that He freely allows us to possess. Neither would we be able to use those resources to purchase those "things" that only satisfy our longings for a short amount of time.

I am by no means suggesting that we are not to have family times, relaxation, outings, or vacations or to be a blessing to others. I believe that God desires for us to do all of that and then some. However, I also believe that a little self-examination is needed so that we can be assured that we are doing His perfect will and not His permissive will. Are we really doing what God wants us to do with the resources that He gives to us? Let's take a look at our spending habits, ask Jesus for His guidance, and stay on that path. Perhaps we should try to focus more on His will and not ours. Until next time, make it a blessed week.

WEEK 26
Let's Remember the Lord

The LORD your God is bringing you into a good land. It has streams and pools of water. Springs flow in its valleys and hills. It has wheat, barley, vines, fig trees, pomegranates, olive oil and honey. There is plenty of food in that land. You will have everything you need. Its rocks have iron in them. And you can dig copper out of its hills. When you have eaten and are satisfied, praise the LORD your God. Praise him for the good land he has given you. Make sure you don't forget the LORD your God. Don't fail to obey his commands, laws and rules. I'm giving them to you today. But suppose you don't obey his commands. And suppose you have plenty to eat. You build fine houses and settle down in them. Your herds and flocks increase their numbers. You also get more and more silver and gold. And everything you have multiplies. But remember the LORD your God. He gives you the ability to produce wealth. That shows he stands by the terms of his covenant. He promised it with an oath to your people long ago. And he's still faithful to his covenant today. (Deut. 8:7-13,18 NIRV)

From time to time, unfortunately, we can all forget the Lord and what He has done for us. When the storms of life seem to overwhelm us or when our spouses, children, coworkers, colleagues, and other family members act not quite as we expect them to, we can and will call upon the Lord constantly. However, when the storms calm down and life gets back on track, when we get the promotion we wanted, the new car, or that new outfit we have been admiring for the last couple of weeks and all seems to be going well in our lives, we can forget who is doing it.

Beloved, we can accomplish nothing of ourselves; we have no power except from Jesus to obtain wealth. The above scripture tells us who is bringing us into our goodness and reminds us to Praise Him. Nothing comes by happenstance. As anointed, appointed, saved, sanctified, intelligent, well-versed, and full of the Holy Ghost as we are, it all happens because of Jesus. If it was not for Jesus's love, mercy, grace, longsuffering, goodness, kindness, and favor, none of us would have what we have or be what we are today. So, that being said, as we continue to progress and accomplish things in this world, let's not forget the Lord! Until next time, make it a blessed week.

WEEK 27

Christ Is Present in Our Storms. Can You See Him?

After he had dismissed them, he went up on a mountainside by himself to pray. When evening came, he was there alone, but the boat was already a considerable distance from land, buffeted by the waves because the wind was against it. During the fourth watch of the night Jesus went out to them, walking on the lake. When the disciples saw him walking on the lake, they were terrified. "It's a ghost," they said, and cried out in fear. But Jesus immediately said to them: "Take courage! It is I. Don't be afraid." (Matt. 4:23–27 NIV)

When it comes to the weather, men and women can predict storms from time to time, including when they will come, their severity, what will possibly happen during them, how we should prepare, and when they will end. However, occasionally they are wrong. A storm can and has caught them by surprise because it does not show up on their radars. There is one person who always knows when the storms will come and when they will end. His radar is fine-tuned to all of life's trials. We should be reminded of His constant presence in the midst of our storms. Jesus knows where the storm is coming from, how we will react or respond during it, what we will learn from it, how long it will last, and the exact fraction of the second it will end. My question is can we see Him?

We all have different storms; some have just a few bumps that toss us to and fro, while others are hit with big waves that try to take us under. The severity or lack thereof does not matter. Jesus always speaks and tells us to *take courage*. There is no need for us to react to the circumstance as if we are alone in it. Instead, we should seek the face of our Master and learn how to respond. There is a difference between reacting and responding, and we need to know what it is.

Beloved, storms will always come into our lives, but we can be assured that our Savior will be in the midst of each one. Whatever you may be facing today or wherever you may find yourself in this Christian journey, remember that Christ is with you. Can you see Him? Until next time, make it a blessed week.

WEEK 28
Lose Yourself and Let You Go

For I have come to turn "a man against his father, a daughter against her mother, a daughter-in-law against her mother-in-law—a man's enemies will be the members of his own household.'

"Anyone who loves their father or mother more than me is not worthy of me; anyone who loves their son or daughter more than me is not worthy of me. Whoever does not take up their cross and follow me is not worthy of me. Whoever finds their life will lose it, and whoever loses their life for my sake will find it." (Matt. 10:35-39 NIV)

Beloved, all of us—sometimes me especially—desire to hold on to that which our Lord and Savior desires for us to let go. Reread the above scripture and ask yourself what or who it is that you are holding on to that God desires for you to let go.

As my husband and I continue to provide marriage and relationship mentoring, we are finding more and more people who are holding on to past hurts, problems, mistakes, doubts, worries, and sins that God sent Jesus to eradicate. I do not know why some of us feel that we are unworthy of receiving the gifts God intended for us to have, one of which is total forgiveness. However, I do know that His word is truth. Some of our hardest trials may be in our households or with our loved ones. For those of us who have prayed and labored before the Lord for our parents and children and they have submitted, bless God for their turnaround. For those who are still agonizing over that wayward child or parent with whom it seems you just cannot get along, release yourself and give them into the hands of the Master, who can and will bring them to Him, though only in His timing and with the surrendering of their wills.

We need to learn to lose ourselves and give the Father freedom to do only that which He can do. Remember, only those who lose their lives because of Jesus will find them. It may be the most difficult trial you will ever have to endure, but trust Jesus. You can do all things through Him. Until next time, make it a blessed week.

WEEK 29

Lord, Help Us Not to Doubt Your Command
(No Matter Who Delivers It)

Now Naaman, captain of the host of the king of Syria, was a great man with his master, and honorable, because by him Jehovah had given victory unto Syria: he was also a mighty man of valor, but he was a leper. And the Syrians had gone out in bands, and had brought away captive out of the land of Israel a little maiden; and she waited on Naaman's wife. And she said unto her mistress, Would that my lord were with the prophet that is in Samaria! then would he recover him of his leprosy. And one went in, and told his lord, saying, Thus and thus said the maiden that is of the land of Israel. And the king of Syria said, Go now, and I will send a letter unto the king of Israel. And he departed, and took with him ten talents of silver, and six thousand pieces of gold, and ten changes of raiment. And he brought the letter to the king of Israel, saying, And now when this letter is come unto thee, behold, I have sent Naaman my servant to thee, that thou mayest recover him of his leprosy. And it came to pass, when the king of Israel had read the letter, that he rent his clothes, and said, Am I God, to kill and to make alive, that this man doth send unto me to recover a man of his leprosy? but consider, I pray you, and see how he seeketh a quarrel against me. And it was so, when Elisha the man of God heard that the king of Israel had rent his clothes, that he sent to the king, saying, Wherefore hast thou rent thy clothes? let him come now to me, and he shall know that there is a prophet in Israel. So Naaman came with his horses and with his chariots, and stood at the door of the house of Elisha. And Elisha sent a messenger unto him, saying, Go and wash in the Jordan seven times, and thy flesh shall come again to thee, and thou shalt be clean. But Naaman was wroth, and went away, and said, Behold, I thought, He will surely come out to me, and stand, and call on the name of Jehovah his God, and wave his hand over the place, and recover the leper. Are not Abanah and Pharpar, the rivers of Damascus, better than all the waters of Israel? may I not wash in them, and be clean? So he turned and went away in a rage. And his servants came near, and spake unto him, and said, My father, if the prophet had bid thee do some great thing, wouldest thou not have done it? how much rather then, when he saith to thee, Wash, and be clean? Then went he down, and dipped himself seven times in the Jordan, according to the saying of the man of God; and his flesh came again like unto the flesh of a little child, and he was clean. And he returned to the man of God, he and all his company, and came, and stood before him; and he said, Behold now, I know that there is no God in all the earth, but in Israel: now therefore, I pray thee, take a present of thy servant. (2 Kings 5:1_15 ASV)

I realize that the above scripture is long. However, I wanted to remind you of the entire story of Naaman and his condition. Leprosy was a terrible disease in those days, and it kept people hidden from their families and surroundings. Sometimes, when we are engulfed with what seems to be an overwhelming circumstance or illness, we want God to handle it our way. My beloved, that is not going to happen. Each of us has a way that we think is better than someone else's. After all, we do know what is best for us and our families, don't we? Or do we?

God's word never changes, but His methods do. We would be wise to remember that what worked yesterday will not necessarily work today, even if it is the same scenario. Or better yet, because it worked for someone else does not mean that it will work for you or me. Remember, we are all fashioned differently.

Because we are sons and daughters of Christ, we should—and I do say should—realize that He is a God of creativity. He can and will create exactly what you and I need to get our breakthrough by whatever means possible. It is, however, our responsibility to respond to the command without the doubt and analyzing what comes along with it. Just because the Lord does not send the messenger to face us or does not allow us to go to the most elaborate and exclusive hospital or ministry to get what He has for us, that does not mean it will not happen.

Naaman complained about what river to dip in. What difference does it make where it is as long as we are going to receive the same benefits? Since Jesus used some spit and dirt to heal the blind man, what makes us think that He will not do the same for us? It is not what is used but how it is used. The anointing lies in the method of how the person uses what is given to him or her and whether or not he or she follows the instructions. It is not the material itself; it is the obedience to use it as instructed.

Let's not be like Naaman and grumble about the command because it does not suit our plans or lifestyles and therefore miss out on our healing and deliverance. Better yet, let's not miss it because it was delivered by someone we did not expect God to send. We must sometimes come out of our comfort zones in an effort to receive our miracles. We will denounce Naaman's spirit from filling us. Until next time, make it a blessed week.

WEEK 30
What Is Your Mouth Inviting?

Does not wisdom call out? Does not understanding raise its voice? Wisdom takes its stand on high ground, by the wayside where the roads meet, near the gates to the city. At the entrance wisdom sings its song, "I am calling to all of you, and my appeal is to all people. You gullible people, learn how to be sensible. You fools, get a heart that has understanding. Listen! I am speaking about noble things, and my lips will say what is right. My mouth expresses the truth, and wickedness is disgusting to my lips. (Prov. 8:1-7 GW)

People of God, the Bible says that we must get a heart of understanding and tells us to say what is right. My question to each of us, including myself, is if we are speaking the truth at all times. Sometimes we tend to compromise the truth depending on to whom we are speaking. If it is a loved one or someone we admire or want to hold us in high standing, then what? What is your mouth inviting? If you are speaking the truth—not honesty, because there is a difference—then you are inviting truth to avail. However, if you or I speak anything else contrary to God's word, the Bible says, *"A fool's lips bring him strife, and his mouth invites a beating"* (Prov. 18:6 NIV).

I can only speak for myself, but I certainly did not like beatings when I was younger, and I do not like them now. So, that being said, I desire to speak the truth and not allow my mouth to invite a beating, especially from the Lord.

Beloved, we must remember that the right thing to say is always right, regardless of whom we are in front of or the consequences of speaking that truth. Remember, we will be held accountable for every idle word we speak. God's word says that wickedness is disgusting to my lips. Is it disgusting to your lips? If not, then you should ask yourself why. We should make it a practice to remain truthful to ourselves and to others by saying what is right, but we must make sure we can say it with *Love*.

Until next time, make it a blessed week.

WEEK 31

We Are Responsible to Help Them Understand!

Then the disciples came and said to him, "Why do you speak to them in parables?" And he answered them, "To you it has been given to know the secrets of the kingdom of heaven, but to them it has not been given. For to the one who has, more will be given, and he will have abundance, but from the one who has not, even what he has will be taken away. This is why I speak to them in parables, because seeing they do not see, and hearing they do not hear, nor do they understand. Indeed, in their case the prophecy of Isaiah is fulfilled that says: "You will indeed hear but never understand, and you will indeed see but never perceive. For this people's heart has grown dull, and with their ears they can barely hear, and their eyes they have closed, lest they should see with their eyes and hear with their ears and understand with their heart and turn, and I would heal them.' But blessed are your eyes, for they see, and your ears, for they hear. For truly, I say to you, many prophets and righteous people longed to see what you see, and did not see it, and to hear what you hear, and did not hear it. "Hear then the parable of the sower: When anyone hears the word of the kingdom and does not understand it, the evil one comes and snatches away what has been sown in his heart. This is what was sown along the path. As for what was sown on rocky ground, this is the one who hears the word and immediately receives it with joy yet he has no root in himself, but endures for a while, and when tribulation or persecution arises on account of the word, immediately he falls away. As for what was sown among thorns, this is the one who hears the word, but the cares of the world and the deceitfulness of riches choke the word, and it proves unfruitful. As for what was sown on good soil, this is the one who hears the word and understands it. He indeed bears fruit and yields, in one case a hundredfold, in another sixty, and in another thirty." (Matt. 13:11b ESV)

As my husband and I come into contact with more and more of God's people, even seasoned Christians, we are finding that they really do not understand the word of God and the benefits that it affords them. Recently, we were speaking with someone who we know for sure has been in church for more than twenty years, yet that person told us that they could not receive some of the word of God because they thought it did not apply to them. They doubted a lot of what the word has to say about our lives. This, my beloved, is a sad thing to hear and even sadder coming from someone who is supposed to be a seasoned Christian.

That being said, we are indeed responsible to help people like this understand. In the above scripture, Jesus took the time to explain to the disciples why He taught in parables. It was so that all people would have an opportunity to hear the word and understand it. Are we taking the time to help those individuals whom God has placed in our lives to understand? I realize that we have busy lives filled with our families, jobs, ministries, etc., but I also realize that we must take a stand for the Kingdom of God.

There are, and most probably always will be, individuals who are difficult to teach; however, that does not excuse us from our assignments. Those of us who walk in the fivefold ministry, as well as those of us who do not, must at all costs act on the word of God, which states, *"Who then is Paul, and who is Apollos, but ministers by whom ye believed, even as the Lord gave to every man"* (1 Cor. 3:5 KJV)?

We are all ministers of the gospel; the Lord gave it to every man. Each of us is responsible to teach one of us. There is absolutely no getting around it. The word of God in the above scripture states that we have been given the secrets of the kingdom of Heaven. Beloved, it is time right now to help our brothers and sisters to realize that the word of God is real and that it can do anything in every situation and circumstance that we face, except fail. Won't you please make a definite decision today to reach out to those who need some wisdom from you? Tomorrow might just be too late.

Until next time, make it a blessed week.

WEEK 32

Beloved, There Is No Lack Among Us!

David. When he pretended to be insane before Abimelech, who drove him away, and he left. I will extol the LORD at all times; his praise will always be on my lips My soul will boast in the LORD; let the afflicted hear and rejoice. Glorify the LORD with me; let us exalt his name together. I sought the LORD, and he answered me; he delivered me from all my fears. Those who look to him are radiant; their faces are never covered with shame. This poor man called, and the LORD heard him; he saved him out of all his troubles. The angel of the LORD encamps around those who fear him, and he delivers them. Taste and see that the LORD is good; blessed is the man who takes refuge in him. Fear the LORD, you his saints, for those who fear him lack nothing. The lions may grow weak and hungry, but those who seek the LORD lack no good thing. (Ps. 34:1–10 NIV)

As our worlds turn, things happen and it looks as though there is a lack in the land. The above Psalm, however, should assure us that there is no lack among us. I realize that over the last several weeks, we may have seen, heard, and experienced life's changing circumstances more up close and personal than we ever thought possible. I myself have thought, *What in the world is happening to this world that we live in?* It is good to know that we just live in this world and are not affected or infected or a part of it.

The above scripture states that those who look to Him are radiant and that their faces are never covered with shame. My beloved, these are the times when we need to look to Jesus more than ever. His word is truth. He will never leave us or forsake us, and the government is upon His shoulders. Instead of us murmuring and complaining, now is the time for us to position ourselves to be that force upon which someone else can lean. It is our responsibility to continue in our encouragements and comfort of those who are losing faith. All of us weaken at some time or point in our lives. Trust me, I do also. However, we still have to look to the hills from which all of our help comes and ask our Savior to give us the strength to go on.

Remember, God never promised that it would be easy. He only said that He would be with us. Let's remember to fear the Lord with reverence, take refuge in Him, and seek the Lord. When we do, while everything and everybody around us grows weak and hungry, we will lack no good thing! Until next time, make it a blessed week.

WEEK 33
Our Salvation Is from the Lord

I have seen a wicked and ruthless man flourishing like a green tree in its native soil, but he soon passed away and was no more; though I looked for him, he could not be found. Consider the blameless, observe the upright; there is a future for the man of peace. But all sinners will be destroyed; the future of the wicked will be cut off. The salvation of the righteous comes from the LORD; he is their stronghold in time of trouble. The LORD helps them and delivers them; he delivers them from the wicked and saves them, because they take refuge in him. (Ps. 37:35–40 NIV)

While some of us, including me, oftentimes wonder how so many people who do not recognize or acknowledge God continue to prosper and we do not, we must realize that the word of God clearly states that He rains on the just as well as the unjust. As long as people abide by the principles of God's word, it will work for them as well. His word is truth, so as long as anyone saved or unsaved applies the principles, it has to work for them.

However, there is good news. The above scripture clearly tells us that what they do soon passes away and is no more. But for those of us who are blameless and upright because of the shed Blood of Jesus, our future will be one of peace. Isn't that wonderful to know? Sinners and their wickedness, the word says, will be destroyed and cut off.

Now, I am not saying for one moment that we should not pray for these people or take every opportunity afforded to us to do the best we can to lead them to accept Jesus as Lord. However, we cannot make them. It is always going to be our responsibility to help them see and turn from the error of their ways. It is not and will never be God's perfect will for one to perish. What I am saying is that our salvation is righteous and it comes from the Lord, and that, my beloved, is a wonderful concept.

Thank God that Jesus is our stronghold in trouble, that our righteousness comes from the Lord, and that He helps us and saves us and delivers us from the wicked. All we need to do to obtain all of this is to continue to take refuge in Him. I can truthfully say that I am so glad that my salvation is from the Lord. How about you?

Until next time, make it a blessed week.

WEEK 34

Are You in Need of a Shepherd?

A psalm of David. The LORD is my shepherd, I lack nothing. He makes me lie down in green pastures, he leads me beside quiet waters, he refreshes my soul. He guides me along the right paths for his name's sake. Even though I walk through the darkest valley, I will fear no evil, for you are with me; your rod and your staff, they comfort me. You prepare a table before me in the presence of my enemies. You anoint my head with oil; my cup overflows. goodness and love will follow me all the days of my life, and I will dwell in the house of the LORD forever. (Ps. 23:1–5 TNIV)

There are times in my life, and perhaps the same is true for you, when I am really in need of a shepherd. While I am assured that God will never leave me or forsake me, I still need to have reassurance that I lack nothing. One of the above verses reminds me that He refreshes my soul, and there are times when my soul needs refreshing. With the demands of everyday life and hectic schedules, we oftentimes can forget to go and have our souls refreshed.

Beloved, we need to make a habit of stopping long enough to refresh our souls in an effort to stay focused on the journey that is set before us. We must remember, it is not just about us. Many people are assigned specifically to us, and if we forget that we have a shepherd to follow and go to, those people will be lost. While I realize that we cannot and should not try to be all things to all people, God does want us to complete the assignments He gave to us before the foundation of our existence.

It is good to know that He guides me along my path, even in the darkest of valleys, and that I do not have to fear. Neither do you. God will never take us where He will not keep us. God has anointed us for such a time as now, and our cups do indeed overflow. Goodness and mercy are ever before us and following us all the days of our lives. It is a wonderful revelation to know that we have a friend that sticks closer than a brother. Beloved, that should make us shout.

If by chance this devotional finds you today in need of a shepherd, be reminded that the Lord is Your Shepherd and you have everything that you need. You lack absolutely nothing. Until next time, make it a blessed week.

WEEK 35

Are You Opening Your Mouth to the Wrong Person?

So Delilah said to Samson, "Tell me the secret of your great strength and how you can be tied up and subdued." Samson answered her, "If anyone ties me with seven fresh thongs that have not been dried, I'll become as weak as any other man." Then the rulers of the Philistines brought her seven fresh thongs that had not been dried, and she tied him with them. With men hidden in the room, she called to him, "Samson, the Philistines are upon you!" But he snapped the thongs as easily as a piece of string snaps when it comes close to a flame. So the secret of his strength was not discovered. Then Delilah said to Samson, "You have made a fool of me; you lied to me. Come now, tell me how you can be tied." He said, "If anyone ties me securely with new ropes that have never been used, I'll become as weak as any other man." So Delilah took new ropes and tied him with them. Then, with men hidden in the room, she called to him, Samson, the Philistines are upon you!" But he snapped the ropes off his arms as if they were threads Delilah then said to Samson, "Until now, you have been making a fool of me and lying to me. Tell me how you can be tied." He replied, "If you weave the seven braids of my head into the fabric on the loom and tighten it with the pin, I'll become as weak as any other man." So while he was sleeping, Delilah took the seven braids of his head, wove them into the fabric and tightened it with the pin. Again she called to him, "Samson, the Philistines are upon you!" He awoke from his sleep and pulled up the pin and the loom, with the fabric. Then she said to him, "How can you say, 'I love you,' when you won't confide in me? This is the third time you have made a fool of me and haven't told me the secret of your great strength." With such nagging she prodded him day after day until he was tired to death. So he told her everything. "No razor has ever been used on my head," he said, "because I have been a Nazirite dedicated to God from my mother's womb. If my head were shaved, my strength would leave me, and I would become as weak as any other man." When Delilah saw that he had told her everything, she sent word to the rulers of the Philistines, "Come back once more; he has told me everything." So the rulers of the Philistines returned with the silver in their hands. Having put him to sleep on her lap, she called for someone to shave off the seven braids of his hair, and so began to subdue him. And his strength left him. Then she called, "Samson, the Philistines are upon you!" He awoke from his sleep and thought, "I'll go out as before and shake myself free." But he did not know that the LORD had left him. (Judg. 16:6-20 NIV)

My dearly beloved, this is just to let you know that even though we love some people, they really mean us no good. The word of God clearly tells us, "Dear friends, do not believe every spirit, but test the spirits to see whether they are from God, because many false prophets have gone out into the world." (1 John 4:1 NIV).

I, like many of you, would love to believe that all people are happy for me in all of my accomplishments. While I realize and pray that they also realize that I can do nothing of myself, it does not mean that they will rejoice with me. The favor that God has on our lives is His choice. We did not earn it, we do not deserve it, and we certainly cannot pay for it. However, because of God's mercies, He extends it to us as He sees fit. When God extends His favor, it is not by happenstance; it is by choice. And sometimes, if not always, "favor ain't fair."

Some people will rejoice with you and celebrate you. Then there are those who will, as Delilah did, deceive you. Some of the people in our lives are simply jealous of God's favor on us and for whatever reason desire to see us fall. We must be careful to whom we expose some of our gifts that God has allowed us to possess. He kindly put those gifts in each of us to develop for His glory and to be a blessing to His people.

Of course, there are people with whom we can freely share our gifts and accomplishments and dreams, knowing that they will sincerely pray for us and support us in every endeavor. But anytime someone asks us repeatedly how we are successful in one particular area of our lives, that should be a warning sign that he or she is up to something. While I am not suggesting that we keep everything a secret from everybody, I am suggesting that we use wisdom in giving an answer to every question asked.

It is like having an old family recipe. You know, the one that has been passed down from your great great grandma and has the secret ingredient that no one can quite guess. There are times when we will have to guard the treasure within us just like we have guarded that recipe. That one ingredient makes all the difference in the world, and we cannot share it with everybody. We should love everybody but guard our treasures and not open our mouths to give away every secret. It might just destroy us.

Until next time, make it a blessed week.

WEEK 36

When Tempers Roll and Anger Strikes, Somebody Pray for Me!

"In your anger do not sin": Do not let the sun go down while you are still angry, and do not give the devil a foothold.(Eph 4:26-27 - (TNIV) But now you must also rid yourselves of all such things as these: anger, rage, malice, slander, and filthy language from your lips. Col. 3:8 - (TNIV) because our anger does not produce the righteousness that God desires. Therefore, get rid of all moral filth and the evil that is so prevalent and humbly accept the word planted in you, which can save you. James 1:20-21 - (TNIV)

Dearly beloved, my, my, my, the spirit of anger that can, and has, grabbed ahold of some of us, if not all of us, at some time or another is a spirit that we oftentimes do not want to let go. The devil knows just who he can lure into his web and use to act out the entire scene and play it well. Unfortunately for me, he knows when I am most vulnerable, and he probably knows when you are vulnerable also. The problem is, some of us do not realize when we are most vulnerable, and then we let our guard down and resort to the enemy's tactics at the wrong time and place. Sometimes, we might even lose our witness to someone else.

The above scripture in Ephesians warns us not to allow ourselves to sin while we are angry. We should not give the devil the advantage of being right in our lives. It further admonishes us to resolve whatever anger we had during our day before we go to bed at night. I realize that this command can be a challenge, but, beloved, we can do this. With the help of our Savior, we can do all things.

The scripture in Ephesians does not suggest; it *tells* us to get rid of anger before the sun goes down. In Colossians, it tells us to rid ourselves of this spirit. Then in James, it tells us that anger will not produce the righteousness of God and that we are His ministers, so we should be producing that which is right. We have all seen, heard, and read about anger and how that spirit can, if we allow it, take us to a place from which we might not have an opportunity to return. We must remember that there are consequences to every choice we make and every spirit that we give in to. People of God, let's do our very best when tempers roll and anger strikes to stop long enough to ask somebody to please pray for us. Until next time, make it a blessed week.

WEEK 37
The Lord Will Take Care of You

The LORD is my light and my salvation; I will fear no one. The LORD protects me from all danger; I will never be afraid. When evil people attack me and try to kill me, they stumble and fall. Even if a whole army surrounds me, I will not be afraid; even if enemies attack me, I will still trust God. I have asked the LORD for one thing; one thing only do I want: to live in the LORD's house all my life, to marvel there at his goodness, and to ask for his guidance. In times of trouble he will shelter me; he will keep me safe in his Temple and make me secure on a high rock. So I will triumph over my enemies around me. With shouts of joy I will offer sacrifices in his Temple; I will sing, I will praise the LORD (Ps. 27:1-6 GNB)

I wonder how many of us truly believe that the Lord will take care of us. For me, there are times when doubt creeps in and I am consumed with worry, wondering if my life's circumstances and situations will work out for my good. I do thank God for His perfect timing. Just when I think there is no hope and I cannot tie three knots and hold on, God once again in His loving and kind ways will send someone or something to provide a word of comfort and reassurance that He is my protector and that the evil that is set before me will not prevail.

It is good to know that even in our weakest moments—and yes, we all have them—God is there with us to shelter us and keep us safe and secure. His protection never fails. We just need to ask for it and remain faithful in our thoughts and learn to offer Him praise in the midst of every circumstance. Even when it seems like we are surrounded by an army of enemies, my beloved, they cannot attack us if we remain in trust of our Lord. Though trials come at every turn, we must continue to go on.

I do not know where this devotion will find you today, but one thing I do know is that wherever you might be and no matter what situation or circumstance you are facing, it is of no surprise to God. You do not need to be alarmed; you simply need to remind yourself that our sovereign God will keep you and me safe in His temple and secure us on His high rock. Until next time, make it a blessed week.

WEEK 38

You May Be Sent to Pull Down and Not Build Up. Will You Do It?

Everything that happens in this world happens at the time God chooses. He sets the time for birth and the time for death, the time for planting and the time for pulling up, the time for killing and the time for healing, the time for tearing down and the time for building. (Eccles. 3:1–3 GNB)

A message came to me from the LORD. He said, "Before I formed you in your mother's body I chose you. Before you were born I set you apart to serve me. I appointed you to be a prophet to the nations." "You are my LORD and King," I said. "I don't know how to speak. I'm only a child." But the LORD said to me, "Do not say, 'I'm only a child.' You must go to everyone I send you to. You must say everything I command you to say. Do not be afraid of the people I send you to. I am with you. I will save you," announces the LORD. Then the LORD reached out his hand. He touched my mouth and spoke to me. He said, "I have put my words in your mouth. Today I am appointing you to speak to nations and kingdoms. I want you to pull them up by the roots and tear them down. I want you to destroy them and crush them. But I also want you to build them up and plant them." (Jer. 1:4–10 NIRV)

Most of us desire to carry a good word to God's people. You know, something that will encourage their hearts and make them jump and shout. However, that is not always the case. There will be times, and for me there have been many, when we have to deliver a hard word from the Lord, just as Jeremiah was instructed to do. There are kingdoms and nations and sometimes our own households that God wants us to pull up and tear down without fear or hesitation. The question is, are we willing to do it?

Some things, my beloved, must be destroyed and crushed. Perhaps it is an unhealthy relationship that the Holy Spirit has been constantly nudging at your heart about and for whatever reason you have refused to pull it up by its roots and destroy it. You continue to make excuses about the reasons you have to keep the fire burning rather than putting it out. I am not in any way suggesting that this relationship is between husband and wife; however, I am suggesting that it might be a relationship or affair that you know you need to walk away from. It could be something that involves your job, church, family, children, siblings, or parents. Perhaps it is not even a relationship; it could be an unhealthy habit, one that has gotten out of control, or even a thought, a grudge, or perhaps a routine that needs to be rooted out, destroyed, and crushed.

God does not want any of us to stay in a state of disobedience to Him. He knows who He can trust to do His work for Him and not do it haphazardly. None of us can continuously ignore the warning signs of wisdom as she admonishes us to rid ourselves of those things that the Holy Spirit desires for us to destroy. Remember, God sends us to pull up and tear down, but as the last verse in Jeremiah states, He also allows us the opportunity to build up and plant again.

So do not be slothful in your assignment for the Lord. He always gives a time for restoration. Until next time, make it a blessed week.

WEEK 39

Do We Really Make It Our Aim to Be Well Pleasing to God?

He who has prepared us for this very thing is God, who has given us the Spirit as a guarantee. So we are always of good courage. We know that while we are at home in the body we are away from the Lord, for we walk by faith, not by sight. Yes, we are of good courage, and we would rather be away from the body and at home with the Lord. So whether we are at home or away, we make it our aim to please him. For we must all appear before the judgment seat of Christ, so that each one may receive what is due for what he has done in the body, whether good or evil. Therefore, knowing the fear of the Lord, we persuade others. But what we are is known to God, and I hope it is known also to your conscience. (2 Cor. 5:5-11 ESV)

I was reading one of my devotionals not too long ago and read the above scripture from 2 Corinthians chapter 5. I especially focused on verse 9, which reads: *We make it our aim ... to be well pleasing to God (NKJV).* I wonder if that is really a true statement. Do we aim to be well pleasing to God or to man? Do we think about our actions, thoughts, decisions, or responses before we say, think, or do them? Will it please God, or do we try to make an impression on those who are around us at the time or who may be watching us from afar, unbeknownst to us?

Those of us who call ourselves Christians should first desire to please our Heavenly Father. However, in more cases than I care to remember, it has not be exhibited. Because we live in a world with things that are constantly pulling at our spirits to get our attention, oftentimes, we tend to sway in the wrong direction. Focusing on God and what He desires for us can be challenging, but that should still remain our desire as we continue to strive to please our creator instead of the things that have been created by man.

By no means am I suggesting that you do not honor all authority that God has allowed to be over you. What I am suggesting is that we be very careful that we do not value man and his desires more than we value God and His. Only our Savior knows the plans He has for each of us, and sometimes, my beloved, we must stand alone in truth and righteous, no matter the cost.

There may be times we will have to lose something in an effort to gain for Christ. We must remember that only what we do for Christ will last.

In my devotion, which I mentioned earlier, it talked about leaders in a children's ministry who handed out cards for the children's good behavior. As the children collected the cards, they would receive prizes of their choice for exhibiting and remaining good during class. However, when one of the leaders handed an eleven-year-old a card for his good behavior, he denied it. His comment was, "I don't need one. I want to behave well, and I don't need a reward for that." Wow, from the mouths of babes. If we could have those same values and put them into practice, how much more effective we would become?

Let's aim our hearts and minds to be well pleasing to God and only Him, not just for a reward, which we will indeed receive, but because we want to! Until next time, make it a blessed week.

WEEK 40

Are You a Whosoever?

And Jesus answering saith unto them, Have faith in God. For verily I say unto you, That whosoever shall say unto this mountain, Be thou removed, and be thou cast into the sea; and shall not doubt in his heart, but shall believe that those things which he saith shall come to pass; he shall have whatsoever he saith. Therefore I say unto you, What things soever ye desire, when ye pray, believe that ye receive them, and ye shall have them. (Mark 11:22-24 KJV)

My beloved readers, I will be the very first to admit that life has its challenges. Every day can bring a new set of trials, circumstances, and temptations that try to lure us away from the comfort of knowing that God is in control. We hear of someone close to our hearts who has lost a loved one; we turn on the news to hear about typhoons, fire, and floods that are taking place in other parts of the world; we listen to what happened in a school were supposedly innocent children did only what they thought to be correct yet lost their lives. All of those things can influence our relationship with our Heavenly Father if we allow them to.

In spite of all our challenges and life's disappointments, we must remain steadfast and unmovable. Our faith in God must be strong and evident so that others will be able to come to us and receive a word of encouragement in their times of need. Oftentimes for me, it is difficult to keep my faith in tact. I sometimes need a faith checkup to remind myself that God is always faithful, no matter what the trials of life bring my way.

The above scripture reminds us that Jesus said that whosoever shall say unto this mountain, be removed and shall not doubt in his or her heart, it shall come to pass. While the word *shall* is definitely used to refer to a future event, the future is the next second in which we live. I suppose my question would be, are we speaking to the mountains in our lives and in the lives of those whom God brings into our path? We must remain in our faith and confident of what we speak, not of what someone else speaks for us.

What we allow to come out of our mouths will come to pass. In these times, we cannot afford to doubt or grow weak and weary in our faith. It is written that "faith is the substance of things hoped for, the evidence of things not seen." So if we hold fast to our faith and believe that we can speak a thing and it shall come to pass because we can have that of which we speak, then *speak* to it. Remember, Jesus said *whosoever* shall say unto this mountain, not the Pastor, Evangelist, Teacher, mother, father, Apostle, but whosoever.

If you are a whosoever like I am, stop doubting our God-given ability and tell your mountain to *MOVE* Until next time, make it a blessed week.

WEEK 41
What Kind of Giver Are You?

for I didn't shrink from declaring all that God wants you to know. "So guard yourselves and God's people. Feed and shepherd God's flock—His church, purchased with His own blood—over which the Holy Spirit has appointed you as elders. I know that false teachers, like vicious wolves, will come in among you after I leave, not sparing the flock. Even some men from your own group will rise up and distort the truth in order to draw a following. Watch out! Remember the three years I was with you—my constant watch and care over you night and day, and my many tears for you. And now I entrust you to God and the message of His grace that is able to build you up and give you an inheritance with all those He has set apart for Himself." I have never coveted anyone's silver or gold or fine clothes. You know that these hands of mine have worked to supply my own needs and even the needs of those who were with me. And I have been a constant example of how you can help those in need by working hard. You should remember the words of the Lord Jesus: 'It is more blessed to give than to receive.' (Acts 20:27-35 NLT)

The above scripture is Paul's writing, and I would like for us to focus on verses 32–35. First and foremost, Paul says that he places them in God's care to remember His great kindness. Do we give people assurance that we are placing them in the care of God and remind them to remember the Lord's kindness, or are we reminding them of what we did for them? We, as saved as we are, can do nothing of ourselves if God does not allow it.

Paul then states that he never wanted anyone's money or clothes. I believe that Paul was saying, if you gave me money and clothes and I accepted it, I did not ask you to give it to me. When presented with a gift, we should be receptive of it. However, in our giving to someone, we must remember that we only have it to give because of God's grace and mercy.

Then Paul says he worked with his own hands to make a living for himself and his friends. How many of us are working to make a living for anybody else besides our wife, husband, or children? Can we truthfully say that we are working to make a living for a friend? Forget about a loved one who may be experiencing some kind of difficulties. Just a friend? We can sometimes be self-centered, selfish individuals in our giving. The Bible clearly states: *"Remember this: The one who plants few seeds will have a small harvest. But the one who plants a lot will have a big harvest"* (2 Cor. 9:6 ERV).

I suppose my next question is what size harvest do you desire? Or do you want a harvest at all? Paul says that everything he did was to show us how we should work to help everyone who is weak. I for one strongly believe that we should use wisdom in what we give to whom. I also strongly believe the last verse of the scripture above, which says more blessings come from giving than receiving. So, my beloved, let's check our level of giving and to whom. Where are you on the scale? Until next time, make it a blessed week.

WEEK 42

Every Failure Presents an Opportunity. We Just Need to Find It!

There shall not any man be able to stand before thee all the days of thy life: as I was with Moses, so I will be with thee: I will not fail thee, nor forsake thee. But I have prayed for thee, that thy faith fail not: and when thou art converted, strengthen thy brethren. Jesus said unto him, Verily I say unto thee, That this night, before the cock crow, thou shalt deny me thrice. And Peter remembered the word of Jesus, which said unto him, Before the cock crow, thou shalt deny me thrice. And he went out, and wept bitterly. (Josh. 1:5; Luke 22:32; Matt. 26:34,75 KJV)

The way the world views failure is not allowed in the kingdom of Christ. Our Heavenly Father does not see failure in any of us. We are His children, who He loves unconditionally. Just as we do not view our children as failures no matter what they do or don't do, God does not view us as failures either.

The above scripture tells us that God will neither fail us nor forsake us. Beloved, at some point in our lives we all feel like we have failed at something. Whether it is being a good mom or dad, a job not well done, a business venture that collapsed, etc. Perhaps someone in our lives constantly told us that we were failures and we took hold of that and embraced the lie instead of the truth. God has allowed me to stop by for a few moments of your time to remind you that you have not and shall not fail Him.

You remember the parable in Matthew chapter 6—you can read a couple of verses of it above—in which Peter told Jesus that he would not deny Him. However, as the heat was turned up and Peter feared for his life, his story changed. Then Peter remembered what he had promised, and I can only imagine that he felt like a complete failure. However, the story did not end there. After Jesus was resurrected, He called for Peter also, and that, my beloved, is how He will always treat you and me. We cannot fail the Savior, simply because He died for us, which includes all of our inadequacies.

We are not perfect beings and we never shall be. We only serve a perfect

Savior. So if you are feeling like a failure today in any area of your life, look up; Jesus is waiting to restore you and show you that there is no failure in Him. Just as Peter's story did not end in failure, yours and mine will not either. Until next time, make it a blessed week.

WEEK 43
Our Acts of Ingratitude—Help Us, Jesus

Therefore, as God's chosen people, holy and dearly loved, clothe yourselves with compassion, kindness, humility, gentleness and patience. Bear with each other and forgive whatever grievances you may have against one another. Forgive as the Lord forgave you. And over all these virtues put on love, which binds them all together in perfect unity. Let the peace of Christ rule in your hearts, since as members of one body you were called to peace. And be thankful. Let the word of Christ dwell in you richly as you teach and admonish one another with all wisdom, and as you sing psalms, hymns and spiritual songs with gratitude in your hearts to God. And whatever you do, whether in word or deed, do it all in the name of the Lord Jesus, giving thanks to God the Father through him. (Col. 3:12-17 NIV)

All of us, from the pulpit to the back door, have and will at some time or another be ungrateful for what others do for us. Our acts of ingratitude can leave an ugly taste in the mouths of the people who experience them. As saved as we are, we sometimes forget who we are and whose we are. In our busy lives, we tend not to take the opportunity to put on compassion, kindness, or humility, and we forget about gentleness and patience; they do not exist on our to-do lists.

It is God's desire for us to bear with one another and forgive, forgive, forgive, whatever grievances we have against one another. But we do not submit to that command. It is my belief that thankfulness and gratefulness are different. We can say that we are thankful, and perhaps we are, but are we grateful? *Thank you*—I believe these two words are habitually spoken with little or no thought simply because we feel or have learned that is the correct thing to say. Gratefulness, in my opinion, requires a different posture of the heart. Have you checked yours lately?

My beloved, we take so many acts of kindness for granted, thinking that we deserve them because of what we have done for the person who is extending the act. However, no one—and allow me to say that again—*no* one owes us anything. It is only by God's grace that He deals with the hearts of people and they allow Him to so that they can freely give to us.

Ingratitude comes when we allow a spirit of entitlement to overtake us. We expect what we feel others should do for us, just because. We take for granted the kindness of the heart of God's people and forget that they have feelings, needs, and expectations just like we do. To remain in an attitude of gratitude, we must daily check our spiritual walk and the hidden issues of our hearts. Remember, it is written *"for thou only knowest the heart of all the children of men"* *(1 Kings 8:39b KJV)*. Let's watch our acts of ingratitude and remain in a posture of gratefulness.

Until next time, make it a blessed week.

WEEK 44
Do We Have Borrowed Faith?

Now faith is being sure of what we hope for and certain of what we do not see. This is what the ancients were commended for. By faith we understand that the universe was formed at God's command, so that what is seen was not made out of what was visible. (Heb. 11:1-3 TNIV)

I wonder how sure we are of the things that we do not see. I do not mean things like the air we breathe or sitting on a chair, knowing it will support us. It is my belief that those come naturally out of our habitual ways. But how sure are any of us regarding the promises of God? Do we believe Him when He says that He will supply all of our needs? Does our faith wander from time to time?

I know my faith wanders. I see and hear of other people's blessings overtaking them and then I take a look at my own life's circumstances and often wonder what happened and if God forgot me. Of course the answer is *no*. However, that does not negate the fact that from time to time I do think about it. Then there are times when I can hear and experience a supernatural blessing from someone and share in his or her excitement, joy, and praise to God and stand on his or her faith, saying that if God did it for that person, surely He will do it for me because He has no respect of person. That being said, I suppose that from time to time I have borrowed faith.

It is not my desire to doubt neither God nor His word. I know beyond a shadow of a doubt that God's word is true to the letter and that He is very real. However, I do not hesitate to accept that it is because of Him that I breathe, move, and have my being. If He does not breathe through me, then I do not breathe. All of us, I believe, sometimes waver in what we have faith in depending on the day, time, circumstance, and situations that we encounter. To be consistently unwavering in our faith takes a complete dedication of our wills to surrender to God's word and to hold on to it no matter what.

When the storms of life seem so powerful and strong that they knock us off our feet, then we should fall to our knees and be sure that when we get up, we will remain steadfast and unmovable, abounding in the word of the Lord. We do not need to have borrowed faith; we just need to know that the faith of a mustard seed will remove any mountain if we just hold fast and know that if God promised it, He can and will do it. Until next time, make it a blessed week.

WEEK 45

Lord, Help Us to Come Before You, with a Pure Heart!

The earth is the LORD's, and everything in it, the world, and all who live in it; for he founded it upon the seas and established it upon the waters. Who may ascend the hill of the LORD? Who may stand in his holy place? He who has clean hands and a pure heart, who does not lift up his soul to an idol or swear by what is false. He will receive blessing from the LORD and vindication from God his Savior. Such is the generation of those who seek him, who seek your face, O God of Jacob. Selah. (Ps. 24:1-6 NIV)

We all should examine our hearts my beloved from time to time. I know that I have to. I do not mean a quick examination, but rather a thorough one. We have motives and issues of the heart that we do not know about and truthfully do not wish to acknowledge. The word of God says; *"for thou, even thou only knowest the hearts of all children of men."* *I Kings 8:39 (KJV)* We do not know the wickedness that lies dormant in our own hearts.

I looked up the word *pure*, and it means free from contamination, complete, not mixed with any other substance. It is my belief that there are times when we bring requests and petitions to the Lord without asking Him to give us a pure heart before we approach Him. All of us desire to receive blessings from our Savior, but do we desire to purify our hearts before we approach His presence? It is my desire that each of us would work to attain uncontaminated, clean, and wholesome hearts so that we can be used by our Heavenly Father for such times that we live in today.

I remember reading somewhere, "We are where we are for such a time as now, not to make an impression, but to make a difference." In order for us to make a difference in the lives of others, we must first make a difference in our own lives. Our approach must be with a pure heart and clean hands. Until next time, make it a blessed week.

WEEK 46

Are You Ready to Possess the Land?

After the death of the LORD'S servant Moses, the LORD said to Moses' assistant Joshua, son of Nun, "My servant Moses is dead. Now you and all these people must cross the Jordan River into the land that I am going to give the people of Israel. I will give you every place on which you set foot, as I promised Moses. "I have commanded you, 'Be strong and courageous! Don't tremble or be terrified, because the LORD your God is with you wherever you go.'" Then Joshua ordered the officers of the people, "Go through the camp. Tell the people, 'Get your supplies ready. In three days you will cross the Jordan River to take possession of the land the LORD your God is going to give you." (Josh. 1:1-3, 9-11 GW)

I have a question for each of us today: If the Lord spoke to you and told you that everywhere you set your foot He will give it to you, would you believe Him? For some of us, believing God for the impossible comes hard, simply because of the circumstances and tribulations that we have faced in life. However, none of those negate God's promises. His word is still true, and He is more than faithful.

In whatever season you may be currently experiencing, I believe that God is calling you and me to get our supplies ready. We have been waiting for that prophecy, dream, and impartation to take place for many years now, and it seems impossible. Some of us have lost hope; others have just given up and we do not wait in expectancy anymore.

My beloved, the Lord sent this word of encouragement to you today just to let you know that with God all things are possible if you only believe. It does not matter how long it has been, how old you are, or where you might find yourself in life, God is still God, and He will bring to pass those things that He has promised. I too get discouraged from time to time, but I refuse to allow the devil to keep me at the doubting door. We all must pick ourselves up, square our shoulders, strengthen our backs, and stand firm on the promises of our Savior.

In three days, God will allow you to cross over to your promised land. The question is will you have your supplies and be ready to move? Let's possess our land with a willingness to do as God directs. Until next time, make it a blessed week.

WEEK 47

Is There Room in Your Inn?

At that time the Emperor Augustus ordered a census of the Roman Empire. This was the first census taken while Quirinius was governor of Syria. All the people went to register in the cities where their ancestors had lived. So Joseph went from Nazareth, a city in Galilee, to a Judean city called Bethlehem. Joseph, a descendant of King David, went to Bethlehem because David had been born there. Joseph went there to register with Mary. She had been promised to him in marriage and was pregnant. While they were in Bethlehem, the time came for Mary to have her child.

She gave birth to her firstborn son. She wrapped him in strips of cloth and laid him in a manger because there wasn't any room for them in the inn. (Luke 2:1-7 GW)

I must admit, I do not always allow room for the King of Kings and Lord of Lords to enter into my inn. There are days and times when I can feel the prompting of the Holy Spirit to do something or call someone; however, because of my to-do list, I am unwilling to give of myself or my time and I do not submit to those promptings. It is indeed not an act of which I am proud, but I believe we all do it from time to time.

As I pondered the scripture above, I wondered if the people who were occupying the inn really knew for whom they were giving up their warm beds and coziness to for the night, would they have responded differently? I find that when I allow the Holy Spirit to control my thoughts and order my days, those days always turn out better. Our selfishness can and will lead us into thoughts and actions that are not pleasing to our Father. Living constantly under the control of the Holy Spirit allows us to freely give of ourselves no matter how cramped our day may seem.

Unselfish love is the key that opens the door to all of the blessings God has in store for us. We will never know what could have been if just one person had made room in the inn for the King's arrival. My beloved, blessings may not come packaged the way we expect, so let's be sensitive enough to make room in our inn and allow the Holy Spirit freedom there. Until next time, make it a blessed week.

WEEK 48
Time Matters. How Are You Using It?

Is anything too hard for the LORD? I will come back to you next year at this time, and Sarah will have a son." Gen 18:14 (GW) The LORD set a definite time. He said, "Tomorrow I will do this." The next day the LORD did as he said. All the livestock of the Egyptians died, but none of the Israelites' animals died. Exod. 9:5-6 (GW) Scripture saw ahead of time that God would give his approval to non-Jewish people who have faith. So Scripture announced the Good News to Abraham ahead of time when it said, "Through you all the people of the world will be blessed." Gal. 3:8 (GW) But when the right time came, God sent his Son into the world. A woman gave birth to him, and he came under the control of God's laws. Gal.4:4 (GW) God also decided ahead of time to choose us through Christ according to his plan, which makes everything work the way he intends. Eph. 1:11 GW)

All of the above scriptures talk about time; therefore, I am convinced that time does matter to our Savior. Unfortunately, we are not always good time managers. Time management is a key factor that should be included in our everyday lifestyle. To become good managers of anything, we must put it into practice. I am, by nature, one of those people who desire to be on time for whatever assignment God has for me. Am I never late? The answer, of course, is *no!* However, I do strive to improve in that area every day that I am afforded another opportunity.

For some of us, lateness is a part of our makeup. We go to bed late, get up late, and get to work late. (You get the picture). Beloved, this should not be so. Our lives should be examples for others, not a stumbling block for those who watch us and know that we are Christians. I realize that it takes effort to use our time wisely, but remember, practice makes perfect. If you do not regularly watch your time and do your best to perfect it, start today. It is never too late to make a change in the right direction for the betterment of your life and those around you.

God has lavishly given us twenty-four hours in a day, which is more than enough time to spend with Him first and then our husbands or wives, children, jobs, etc., if we learn the strategy of time itself. Again, some of us need to learn to multitask, but that does not mean eating while watching TV; it means putting ourselves on a schedule that will work for us and keeping it for twenty-one days to develop a good habit.

Remember, God has a plan for time, and it matters to Him. Let's be careful how we spend the time that God so willingly gives to His children. The Bible says, *"So teach us to number our days that we may get a heart of wisdom"* *(Ps. 90:12 ESV)*. We can do anything that we set our minds to. But our time does not belong to us. It is the Father's choice to extend it to us each day as we seek Him in how to use it wisely. Let's make a commitment today to know that time matters and to use it well. Until next time, make it a blessed week.

WEEK 49

Are You Working for You or for Jesus?

Neither the wise person nor the fool will be remembered for long, since both will be forgotten in the days to come. Both the wise person and the fool will die. So I came to hate life because everything done under the sun seemed wrong to me. Everything was pointless. It was like trying to catch the wind. I came to hate everything for which I had worked so hard under the sun, because I will have to leave it to the person who replaces me. Who knows whether that person will be wise or foolish? He will still have control over everything under the sun for which I worked so hard and used my wisdom. Even this is pointless. Brothers and sisters, in view of all we have just shared about God's compassion, I encourage you to offer your bodies as living sacrifices, dedicated to God and pleasing to him. This kind of worship is appropriate for you. Don't become like the people of this world. Instead, change the way you think. Then you will always be able to determine what God really wants—what is good, pleasing, and perfect. (Eccles. 2:16-19; Rom. 12:1-2 GW)

I will be the first to admit that there is nothing wrong with work, but who are we working for? Neither is there anything wrong with leaving a legacy or estates to our children or loved ones, but is it more important to us to leave things or to leave a legacy that demonstrates our love and commitment to Christ? Do we really want to be remembered for what we worked to achieve in this world, or do we want our memories to be of the many lives that we touched and made a difference in as we traveled through this journey?

Several months ago, my husband and I attended the funeral of one of our spiritual grandchildren, and although the loss was great and the pain almost unbearable, it was indeed a blessing to have been in his life. The legacy left behind was both rewarding and comforting as we sat and listened to the many people whose lives had been touched by that life. As tears flowed uncontrollably down my cheeks, I listened intently to the many comments from so many people who expressed the love, kindness, words of encouragement, and preaching that our wonderful loved one had left them with. My heart overflowed with gratefulness for the many people who were reached during such a short lived life.

That, my beloved, is the kind of legacy I believe we all should be attempting to leave behind. It is one that will last throughout eternity. We need to check our work ethnic and ask ourselves this question: Who are we working for? Until next time, make it a blessed week.

A Word for Your "Weak"
WEEK 50
When Trouble Comes, God Will Answer!

You, O Lord, are good and forgiving, full of mercy toward everyone who calls out to you. Open your ears to my prayer, O LORD. Pay attention when I plead for mercy. When I am in trouble, I call out to you because you answer me. No god is like you, O Lord. No one can do what you do. All the nations that you have made will bow in your presence, O Lord. They will honor you. Indeed, you are great, a worker of miracles. You alone are God. Teach me your way, O LORD, so that I may live in your truth. Focus my heart on fearing you. I will give thanks to you with all my heart, O Lord my God. I will honor you forever. (Ps. 86:5–12 GN)

It is so comforting to me to know that when trouble comes, and it inevitably will, God will answer. For some of us, it can seem as if trouble has a way of finding us no matter how hard we try to avoid it. For me, there have been seasons that seemed to only bring trouble. However, because I know that the God I serve is greater, I have been able to call upon Him and expect Him to rescue me. My beloved, for me, that is good news.

The psalm writer says that he called upon the Lord because he knew that the Lord would answer him. It is reassuring to know in your spirit that God will indeed redeem us from whatever trial or circumstance we may be facing. Our focus and thoughts must turn first to our sovereign Lord when trouble comes to our door. Friends and family can and have been a support in our times of need; however, none of them, as loving as they are, can or should replace our need for the Master's divine entrance into our situations.

The psalmist says there is no one like our God and no one can do what He does. That is a very profound statement. It should be our prayer for the Lord to teach us to live in His truth. I believe that staying in the presence of the King allows us to refresh and restore our weary souls and come to a place of knowing that absolutely nothing is too hard for our God. That being said, the next time trouble shows up at our doors, we should know that God has already made a way of escape. All we need to do is give the circumstances to Jesus, and He will answer.

Until next time, make it a blessed week.

WEEK 51

Lord, Don't Send Me Without Your "Presence"

And whenever Moses went out to the tent, all the people rose and stood at the entrances to their tents, watching Moses until he entered the tent. As Moses went into the tent, the pillar of cloud would come down and stay at the entrance, while the LORD spoke with Moses. Whenever the people saw the pillar of cloud standing at the entrance to the tent, they all stood and worshiped, each at the entrance to his tent. The LORD would speak to Moses face to face, as a man speaks with his friend. Then Moses would return to the camp, but his young aide Joshua son of Nun did not leave the tent. Moses said to the LORD, "You have been telling me, 'Lead these people,' but you have not let me know whom you will send with me. You have said, I know you by name and you have found favor with me.' If you are pleased with me, teach me your ways so I may know you and continue to find favor with you. Remember that this nation is your people." The LORD replied, "My Presence will go with you, and I will give you rest." Then Moses said to him, "If your Presence does not go with us, do not send us up from here. (Exod. 33:8-15 NIV)

Most of us want presents from God, but not His presence. There is indeed a difference, and we all should seek His presence daily. I cannot speak for any of you, but I do not desire to go anywhere or do anything without the "presence" of the Lord. Our assignments as ministers of the gospel can be difficult, and from time to time we are reluctant to carry them out based on our own strength or lack thereof. However, we must remind ourselves that God does not require us to do anything that He has not already equipped us to do.

Moses was reluctant to lead God's people unless he knew exactly who God was going to send with him. There are times when we may have to go alone and complete a task that might require us to be in an uncomfortable position. However, that does not mean that we are not equipped for the assignment.

My beloved, all we need is God to go with us and we can accomplish any task that He has anointed us to do. I will, however, encourage you to make sure that God has assigned the task and not you or man. When you are certain that the task is from God, then go and there will be a blessing awaiting you. Just remember to ask God to send with you His presence and you will continue to do exceptional work for the Kingdom. Until next time, make it a blessed week.

WEEK 52
Lord, Help Us to Be Trained by Your Discipline!

Endure hardship as discipline; God is treating you as sons. For what son is not disciplined by his father? If you are not disciplined (and everyone undergoes discipline), then you are illegitimate children and not true sons. Moreover, we have all had human fathers who disciplined us and we respected them for it. How much more should we submit to the Father of our spirits and live! Our fathers disciplined us for a little while as they thought best; but God disciplines us for our good, that we may share in his holiness. No discipline seems pleasant at the time, but painful. Later on, however, it produces a harvest of righteousness and peace for those who have been trained by it. (Heb. 12:7–11 NIV)

My beloved brothers and sisters, no one likes discipline. I know that I did not, and even now I sometimes struggle with it. I was not fortunate enough to be brought up in a home with both a mom and dad, but my mom was a disciplinarian. My older brother also gave his opinion of what should be done. I sometimes resented his opinions and objectives, but later I learned to respect them.

I have read about some of the strenuous training Olympic athletes undergo, and I have wondered how long it takes them to accomplish their goals. Training can and is an act of our will. It is amazing to me that we will put a lot of time and energy and money into training for that which we wish to accomplish. But will we allow God to train us to be disciplined by His word?

I will be the first to admit that being a doer of the word is not an easy task, but it can be accomplished. For those of us who can recall the discipline of our natural fathers and mothers, some of us resented that training. But the training of God brings out the best in each of us.

As the scripture above states, our earthly fathers disciplined according to what they thought was best. They only knew what they had been taught, and those values, my beloved, could have been wrong. Everything God allows us to go through is for us so that in the end, He will get the Glory.

He knows our very thoughts, even those far in the future, so He must take steps to correct us by any means possible. Remember, God's discipline brings about righteousness and peace for us if we allow Him to train us according to His will. Submitting to the will of God takes us out of our comfort zones, but the rewards are out of this world.

Some of us feel that we no longer need teaching, so we reject the training. I believe we should desire to remain teachable until Jesus comes. With all of that said, let's open our hearts today and allow the Holy Spirit to train us with a strong arm in the discipline that God has according to His plans and purposes for our lives. Until next time, make it a blessed week.

Notes

Notes

Notes

Notes

_____

_____

_____

_____

_____

_____

_____

_____

_____

_____

_____

_____

_____

_____

_____

_____

Notes

Notes

Notes

Notes

Notes

Notes

Notes

Notes

Notes

Notes

_____

_____

_____

_____

_____

_____

_____

_____

_____

_____

_____

_____

_____

_____

_____

Notes

Notes

Notes

Notes

Notes

Notes

Notes

Notes

Notes

_____

_____

_____

_____

_____

_____

_____

_____

_____

_____

_____

_____

_____

_____

_____

Notes

Notes

Printed in the United States
By Bookmasters